SHERBORN
& THE
IN THE Tₙₘₑ ᴏꜰ
JANE AUSTEN

WITH AN ACCOUNT OF THEIR
EARLIER HISTORY

RUPERT WILLOUGHBY

© Rupert Willoughby 2002
Designed and published by the author at
The Old Rectory, Sherborne St John,
Hants., RG24 9JD

Printed by Creeds the Printers,
Broadoak, Bridport, Dorset DT6 5NL

ISBN 0 9534428 3 7

Front cover: William John Chute: pastel attributed to Emma Smith. Described as 'a fine specimen of the real old English squire,' Chute loved Sherborne St John, but stood stubbornly in the way of much-needed modernisation. (Courtesy of the NTPL/Derrick E. Witty.)

Centre pages: George Wither's plan of Beaurepaire Park and Grounds, dated 28 July 1613. It depicts a network of roads in the north part of the parish that has largely vanished. Beaurepaire Mill and The Vyne are familiar landmarks, as is 'Dickensons house', identifiable as Hillend Farm.

Back cover: Sketch by Caroline Wiggett of the Square, Sherborne St John, dated 1813. The house with a jettied upper floor, near the disused maypole and stocks, has been transformed into the modern Haye. Then a humble pair of cottages, it changed hands in 1818 for the equivalent of twenty-five pence. Next to it is the old cottage on the site of the present Post Office. On the extreme right-hand side of the picture, the then open stream that crossed the village street disappears under a malthouse attached to Edernish House, which in those days was known as 'Tally's'. (Courtesy of the Hampshire Record Office. The sketch is taken from an old album in the Chute collection - ref. 31 M57/652.)

The Vyne in Hampshire, former seat of the Chute family, is one of the finest and best-known Tudor mansions in England. Much has been written of the house and its contents: they were bequeathed to the National Trust by Sir Charles Chute, who died in 1956. The untold story is that of the surrounding parish, and of its relations with The Vyne over many centuries.

Originally the palatial residence of Lord Sandys, a favourite of Henry VIII, The Vyne has received many famous visitors, including Elizabeth I and Sir Walter Ralegh. Reduced in scale by the Chutes, it seemed to be almost forgotten by time. Virtually unreachable by road, it descended into an obscure country seat, all but invisible under a thick covering of ivy.

The parish of Sherborne St John, which had prospered from the nearness of a medieval priory and from the patronage of the Sandys family, had in the process become a stultifying, forsaken backwater. Its neglect was never more evident than in the lordship of William John Chute (1757 - 1824), whose life and times have been documented in extraordinary detail. An unusual if attractive personality, Chute was uncomfortable with all forms of change, which he resisted to the utmost. His inertia was matched by that of his feudally-minded neighbour, Mrs Brocas of Beaurepaire, with whom he shared a controlling interest in the parish.

By focusing on Chute, this book opens a window on the whole rich past of Sherborne St John, before the obliteration, in the 19th century, of much of its ancient fabric. Wry and controversial, it is the story of two great houses and of many lesser ones; of high art juxtaposed with the vernacular; of significant events and of daily routine; of masters and servants; of rich folk, and of the abundant poor.

FOR ARTHUR AND ATALANTA -
BOTH BORN IN SHERBORNE ST JOHN

Contents

SHERBORNE ST JOHN
& THE VYNE
IN THE TIME OF
JANE AUSTEN

Introduction

Not the least of the splendid monuments in Westminster Abbey is that to Sir Bernard Brocas. Lifelong friend and companion in arms of the Black Prince, Sir Bernard is represented, in a wooden carving on his tomb, as a recumbent figure in armour. Upon his helmet is the family crest, the Moor's head with an oriental crown. The arms on his shield are a golden lion, ramping in a field of black. Sir Bernard was lord of Beaurepaire in the parish of Sherborne Saint John, and the same crest continues to be much in evidence in the locality - on the gate-posts to the moat bridge at Beaurepaire, on brasses in the parish church, and on the weathercocks above the Brocas Aisle at the church of neighbouring Bramley.

Sir Bernard's tomb has long been a favourite among visitors to the Abbey. He used to be pointed out to them as 'the lord who had cut off the the the king of Morocco's head'. In reality, the Moor's head, crowned or otherwise, is a standard heraldic device, and there is no evidence that he had fought with any real Moorish adversary, let alone a king.

In one of Addison's essays in *The Spectator*, published in the early 1700s, the fictional Sir Roger de Coverley is himself taken on a tour of the Abbey, and listens with particular interest to the verger's account of Sir Bernard. As the archetype of the conservative country squire, it is curious that Sir Roger should come to life, a hundred years later, in the person of William John Chute, whose seat at The Vyne was also in Sherborne St John, within a mile of the Brocas house at Beaurepaire. Comparisons were drawn at the time. Descriptions of Sir Roger could certainly be applied, word for word, to Chute, who was 'cheerful, gay, and hearty; keeps a good house in both town and country; a great lover of mankind; but there is such a mirthful cast in his behaviour, that he is rather beloved than esteemed'. Like Sir Roger, the real squire was 'very singular in his behaviour', his singularities being 'contradictions to the manners of the world'. However, 'this humour creates him no enemies, for he does nothing with sourness or obstinacy'. A foible of both men was their wearing into old age the fashions of their youth. Chute further emulates his model by living on terms of easy familiarity with his servants, although his 'humanity and good nature engages everybody to him'. They were never more alike than in church, with both men keeping a watchful eye on their tenants, and insisting on their attendance, although in neither instance was there much spiritual edification in the experience.

The blissful situation of being a country squire encouraged many notable eccentrics. A few miles from Sherborne, at Deane, members of the Harwood family made a similar impression, one of them being supposedly the model for Squire Western in *Tom Jones*. (Its author, Fielding, used to stay at Oakley Hall.) A later John Harwood was, incidentally, to become Rector of Sherborne. William Chute may also have inspired a novelist, in his case Jane Austen, a family friend (and sister of the then Vicar of Sherborne), who is unusual among contemporaries in speaking ill of him. Whilst characters as vivid and colourful as Harwood or Chute are the stock-in-trade of imaginative writers, they turn up but rarely in the pages of history. Their mark on the world is usually ephemeral, depending not on high deeds but on minute details of speech, dress or comportment. The memory of William Chute was not, however, destined to fade, but to live on in the accounts of his contemporaries, principally the *Reminiscences* of his niece, Caroline Workman (1869-70), her brother Wiggett Chute's *Notes on the Vyne and Property* (1872), and Edward Austen-Leigh's *Recollections of the Early Days of the Vine Hunt* (1868).

These precious sources (of which only Austen-Leigh's has been committed to print) evoke not only the personality of William Chute, but the world in which he lived, particularly the parish of Sherborne St John, which he mostly owned. In combination with other evidence, they bring to life a lost world, for the landscape of Sherborne and the fortunes of its inhabitants have now, in most respects, been changed beyond recognition. Personalities, fashions, modes of speech, individual houses and cottages, even the experience of attending church, can all be re-created and described in extraordinary detail. The present book is therefore the story of William John Chute, but of much more besides.

The Vyne is of course central to the story. As is historically proper, though, equal weight is given to neighbouring Beaurepaire, a house of similar size and antiquity, which for five centuries was seat to the older and much more illustrious family of Brocas. For want of a male heir, the estate was sold in 1873, along with all its contents, and has since passed through various hands. The mansion-house, entirely rebuilt in about 1760, was gutted by fire during the Second World War. Only a corner of the former structure survives, and this has been incorporated by the present owners into the modern building, a *tour de force* by the architect Tom Bird. With its medieval moat and park still intact, it remains a place of extraordinary beauty and seclusion.

Incidentally, the name 'Beaurepaire' was always pronounced 'Beroper' or 'Baroper', and is often so spelt in old documents. No self-respecting Englishman, at least since the Middle Ages, would have attempted to utter it like a Frenchman. Monsieur Lyon, the Huguenot refugee who became Vicar of Sherborne in 1699, would no doubt have pronounced it perfectly, as, on occasion, might William Chute, a notable impersonator of the French. For everyone else, 'Beaurepaire', like 'Beaulieu', 'Belvoir' and 'Beauchamp', had been stubbornly adapted to the English tongue. The traditional pronunciation of 'Sherborne' is also evident from old documents, where it appears as 'Sherburn' or even 'Sherbon'. The 'burn' from which it is named has been known variously as the Weybrook or the Sher since medieval times. The latter name, current in the early twentieth century, is seldom if ever heard today. Finally, it may be mentioned that the modern spelling of The Vyne is an affectation, apparently in use by 1793. That is how it appears in the earliest diaries of William Chute's wife, Eliza, whereas Horace Walpole, a generation before, writes of 'the Vine'. Like its mantle of ivy, the old-fashioned spelling was thought by the romantically-minded to lend it an appropriate air of antiquity.

CHAPTER ONE

'A Mouldering Estate'

i   Brushwood and Venison

Sherborne Saint John is as old a community as any in England. The Saxons, enchanted by the pure waters of the Weybrook, first spoke of it as the 'Scir bourn' or bright stream, but Romans had lived here before them and known the place by another name.

In medieval times, if not before, the settlement had taken its distinctive shape, that of a row of dispersed hamlets and isolated farmsteads, each originating as a clearing in a seemingly endless expanse of forest. That forest after 1066 was the Royal Forest of Pamber, the jealously protected preserve of the King, who cherished, with a passion, the sport that was to be had there. Not a branch could be cut, nor any wild creature killed, without his licence. The interests of the deer were set firmly above those of his subjects, whose natural desires to exploit the land, to hunt and to put fresh game on their tables were ferociously suppressed in his specially-created forest courts. About a third of the kingdom was so affected, and the forests were nowhere more numerous than in Hampshire and Berkshire.

Encroachments over time, licensed or otherwise, had nevertheless reduced the boundaries of Pamber Forest and had freed Sherborne from the strict application of the detested forest law. William de Saint John (great-great-grandson of Hugh de Port, to whom William the Conqueror had granted both the east and west parts of Sherborne) had carved out a park of his own within the 'metes' of the forest, which he had enclosed 'with a dike and hedge'. Only one of the most powerful barons in the land could have acted so high-handedly; only an indulgent king like Henry III would have allowed it.

William's park, for which his son obtained official recognition in 1245, was called Morgaston Wood. For his part, Robert de Saint John piously promised to donate 'the right shoulder of every deer' that he killed there to the nearby Benedictine Priory. This had been founded by Henry de Port in the 1120s, as a place where his own family could be buried and their souls prayed for. The original colony is thought to have been settled at All Saints' Church in West (now Monk) Sherborne, apparently a much larger building in those days, for there are traces of an apse beyond the chancel. Later, the dozen or so monks and their Prior had been relocated in a purpose-built complex, partially surrounded by a moat, at Pamber End. The present Priory Church, part of the united benefice of the Sherbornes with Pamber, is all that remains of it, together with earthworks on three sides that are vestiges of the former moat.

Sherborne Priory was a daughter house of the community of St Vigor at Cerisy, near Bayeux and within easy reach of Port-en-Bassin, the ancestral home of the Ports. William de Saint John was the son of Adam de Port but took the surname of his mother's family, to which she was heiress. The sepulchral slabs of the Ports and Saint Johns and their friends, made of expensive Purbeck marble, are still to be seen in the Priory Church, though they have been repositioned. In a recess in the western wall, another member of the family is commemorated by an oak effigy, which is thought to date from the late 1200s.

The striking tower of the Priory Church, with its narrow windows, is typically Norman, and other features seem to have been borrowed from the parent house at St Vigor. The interior walls were plastered over and gaudily painted (there are traces of bright red paint and of an elaborate mural depicting five angels), as would be expected in any important building of the period. Some idea of this can be gained at Bramley Church, a possession, though only a minor one, of the medieval Priory, where a Victorian vicar was happily to rediscover a riot of contemporary wall decorations under a layer of whitewash.

The missing structures of the monastery included guest lodgings that were frequently used by King Henry III and his Queen. Their regular journeys between Reading or Windsor and Winchester might be broken at the Priory for a day or two at a time, an opportunity for some hunting in the Forest as well as for the routine royal business of issuing writs. In 1249, Henry donated an oak from the Forest which was for 'making the windows in the Queen's chamber there'. There are records from the 1250s of his replenishing the cellar at Sherborne Priory, as at other regular stops on his itinerary, including Chawton; and of further donations of oak, for use in rebuilding the roof of the church.

The Priory appears to have prospered mightily during this period. From the late thirteenth century, it was increasingly neglected by its former patrons, and by the 1380s was in sharp decline. The last monks were evicted in 1452 in favour, eventually, of Queen's College, Oxford, who own the Priory estates to this day. The monks must ever have been aware of their dependency and of the inviolability of the Forest. The haunches of venison from Morgaston Wood had kept coming, at least for a while; but even to collect brushwood for their hearth from the encircling Pamber Forest had required the express permission of the King. Whole trees for their fire were only occasionally and perhaps grudgingly given in Henry's reign.

ii   Vyne Green

East Sherborne, known by the fourteenth century as Sherborne St John, can only have benefited from the proximity of such a place. The Priory would have been a major source of employment, not least to builders, and of alms from its almonry. Brothers are bound to have been recruited from the local community, and boys of the humblest background would thus have been assured of a secure and comfortable future, to the advantage of their entire family.

Henry de Port's original endowment had included 'the mill next to the fishpond and the meadow' in East Sherborne. The mill at Mill End has a long history and was operational until the late 1920s; it was later dismantled, and the adjacent mill pool has been filled in. (There were other old mills - Domesday Book refers to three - at Beaurepaire and at The Vyne, at the outfall of the lake.) Adam de Port was subsequently to repossess the mill in exchange for a gift of tithes. Whilst the whole of West Sherborne, including its church, had been given over to the monks, the lords had clearly preferred to keep East Sherborne, including its parish church, for themselves.

Henry or John de Port had rebuilt the Church of St Andrew in the mid-1100s. Three sides of the Norman nave survive to this day, together with the font. (The parish priest appears to have been, *ex officio,* a senior dean at the Priory, and the parish was also known in the fourteenth century as Sherborne Dean.) In addition, John de Port founded and endowed a Chantry Chapel next to his manor-house here, which was on or near the site of The Vyne. The chapel was for the convenience of his retainer, William FitzAdam, who lived here for many years, and died soon after 1202: Sherborne was probably rarely if ever used by the lords themselves, their chief residence being nearby, at Basing Castle.

The early manor-house, long thought to have been across the road from the present one, was known by at least 1268 as 'The Vyne'. According to Camden in his *Britannia* (1586), it had been the site of the first Roman vineyard in this country, in the time of the Emperor Probus (A.D. 276 - 282). The sub-manor of Sherborne Cowdray which formed around it - named after the knightly family which occupied it in the thirteenth and fourteenth centuries - had probably developed from a Saxon 'denn', a clearing in the forest for summer pasture. In 1268, the whole of Sherborne was still well within the bounds of Pamber Forest. Peter de Cowdray obtained a licence in that year to enclose Cufaude ('Cowfold') Wood: this, his second deer park, was north-east of the present house, around what is now Vyne Lodge Farm.

The Cowdray estate passed in 1355 to the Fyfhides of Fifield, near Andover, but the manor-house was said in 1362 to be 'of no value beyond the outgoings'. It was promptly leased to one William Gregory of Basingstoke, who covenanted to maintain 'the hall, and the adjoining chambers, and the grange, and the Chapel at the house'. In 1386, Sherborne

Cowdray was acquired by Sir John Sandys, from Cholderton, who had married the Fyfhide heiress.

The great-great-grandson of this couple, William, Lord Sandys, succeeded to the property in 1496. 'At the tyme,' wrote a contemporary, 'ther was no very great or sumptuous Maner Place, and was only conteinid within the mote.' A corner of the 'old moat' has traditionally been pointed out across the road, opposite the Stables. Recent theories are that the small pond in question is the remains not of a moat but of a clay pit, and that Sandys developed the existing site. The present Vestibule and Staircase Hall, which are enclosed by unusually thick walls, may even incorporate the medieval hall.

Whatever the truth of the matter, Sandys transformed his insignificant patrimony into one of the greatest houses in the country, a rival to nearby Basing House and to Hampton Court itself. The surviving main range of The Vyne represents merely a third of what was here before. A complex of inter-connected buildings extended on the north side - then and long afterwards regarded as the front of the house - to the very edge of the water. The buildings here were a full storey lower than the central block, which stands on higher ground. They were grouped around as many as four inner courtyards, the largest of which was described as 'a fair Base Court'. The gabled, two-storey blocks around the Base Court included lodgings for the schoolmaster, the cook, and the yeomen of the household. Another room served as an Armoury. There are no traces of an approach road from the north, but access to the mansion was by means of a gatehouse and bridge across the Weybrook, which had not then been widened into a lake. On the farther bank there was a formal garden, which included a bowling green.

The long walk through the Base Court to the State Rooms on the hill was designed to be, in every sense, breathtaking. Henry VIII and his Queen, Ann Boleyn, were guests here in October 1535. They came for a long weekend (Friday to Tuesday) and used the bedrooms on either side of the Oak Gallery. (The Queen is said to have been put up in the Tapestry Room in the tower whilst the King was in the now-partitioned Gallery and South Bedrooms above the Strawberry Parlour and Print Room.) Elizabeth I was entertained here, too, in 1569: a letter survives which she sealed 'at the manor of the Vine'. No doubt she was much distracted by the affairs of Mary, Queen of Scots, but in no other private house would she have seen so splendid a chapel (the woodwork is superb and the stained glass is rivalled only by that at King's College, Cambridge) nor any decoration so rich as that in the Oak Gallery (barely altered since and the finest of the few surviving long galleries in England).

The Tudor Vyne would have been like a small town, and the members of the household numbered in hundreds. In their Base Court lodgings, for example, there were twenty-four beds for the yeomen. Moreover, the manor-house was then, and perhaps always had been, on the edge of a small hamlet. It was called Vyne Green. The only remaining house there, Vyne Farm, dates from 1695 and was originally called New Farm. It is probably therefore on the site of the 'New Inne lying in le Vyne Grene next to [the] manor of le Vyne', documented in 1537. If there was a green in between (with at least half a dozen houses around it), it would explain why the manor-house is set at a curious angle from the road.

iii   Questions of Taste

The fate of the Vyne Green cottages is not recorded, but the greater part of the mansion-house was demolished in 1654 by its new owner. The Sandys family had declined in both wealth and power, and were soon to die out altogether. William, 4th Lord Sandys had sold the estate in 1653 to Chaloner Chute, a Middle Temple barrister, sometime Knight of the Shire for Middlesex, and Speaker in the last Parliament of the Commonwealth, when he was held by virtue of his office to be 'the greatest man in England'. Chute was a brilliant, fearless and successful lawyer, with a delightfully relaxed attitude to his profession: 'if he had a fancy not to have the fatigue of business, but to pass his time in pleasure after his own humour, he would say to his clerk, "Tell the people, I will not practise this term," and was as good as his word ... I guess that no Chancery practiser ever did, or will do, the like; and it shows a transcendent genius, superior to the slavery of a gainful profession.'

Among Chute's more agreeable distractions were no doubt his plans to consolidate and beautify his Hampshire estate, for which task he recruited the Palladian architect John Webb. Having obliterated the redundant Base Court, he tidied up the north façade of the remaining main block, into which he incorporated a Corinthian portico, the first on any country house in England. The old mullioned windows were replaced by sashes, a further novelty, as these were generally introduced (from Holland) in the reign of William III. Chute built the summer-house in the garden and installed new floors and chimney-pieces, and might have done much more. He died on his estate at Chiswick in 1659, exhausted by his office, without ever having been able to take up permanent residence at The Vyne.

The Speaker's immediate descendants, who did live there, were content to keep the house as he had left it. A grandson, Edward, fitted the lead stack pipes which bear the initials of himself and his wife, Katherine; a lead cistern near the side entrance is similarly marked and dated 1696. At The Vyne, even such mundane objects are beautiful! Their son Anthony imported large quantities of furniture from the makers Vile and Cobb. The property seems otherwise to have been neglected until, in 1754, it was inherited by John Chute, Anthony's youngest brother. After an education at Eton, John Chute had spent much of his life abroad, living principally in Florence, where he had freely indulged his aesthetic predelictions. As he dutifully made his way home, he had commented that he was 'not able to find the least comfort in being one horrid step nearer to a mouldering estate'.

One can readily imagine the expression of patient suffering on John's face as he rattled up the lane to his inheritance, his beloved black cat, Polleri, on his knee. The Vyne was no longer the resort of statesmen and kings, was notoriously damp, and was difficult to reach, the approach roads having fallen into an appalling state of disrepair. John made the prospect of living there bearable by planning ambitious improvements to the house. At Florence, in 1740, he had first met Horace Walpole, son of the Prime Minister, along with

Walpole's Eton contemporary, the poet Thomas Gray. Whether or not it was love at first sight, Walpole and John Chute, sixteen years his senior, had formed a life-long attachment. As a member of Walpole's 'Committee of Taste', John had been able at Strawberry Hill, his friend's 'little Gothic castle', to put some of his architectural theories into practice. In return, Walpole took a keen interest in his plans for The Vyne, and was a frequent visitor. Their most ambitious proposals never came to pass. An expert on heraldry and genealogy, John created the Tomb Chamber on the side of the Chapel (perhaps in place of a former Vestry), as a memorial to his distinguished ancestor, the Speaker; and he enlarged the lake probably to its present size, which would have been at the expense of the formal gardens on the farther bank; but his main contribution was the magnificent, classical-style Staircase, which he personally designed. John Chute died in 1776, leaving £300 to the poor of Sherborne St John. The residual heir, his cousin Thomas Lobb, was left a thousand-pound bill for the Tomb Chamber; and Walpole lamented the loss of his 'other self'.

Thomas Lobb's mother, Elizabeth, had been John's first cousin, the daughter of Thomas Chute, who had settled in Norfolk, at Pickenham Hall, in about 1700. It must have pained John to be the last of nine brothers and sisters, all of whom were childless, but he was determined that the house of Chute should live on. As enjoined in his will, Thomas duly adopted the surname in addition to that of Lobb. He did nothing to the house, however, other than finish off the Tomb Chamber, to which he was rather unwillingly committed. He was quite happy to remain at Pickenham, and was buried there in 1790.

Sheer neglect on the part of successive squires had had a devastating effect on the estate and on Sherborne St John in general. The roads were simply dreadful. Walpole confined his visits strictly to the summer months: 'In October you will find it a little difficult to persuade me to accompany you there on stilts,' he told a friend. To another he wrote: 'No post but a dove can come from thence'. In a subsequent letter, he fears that John Chute will 'die of mildew'. Thomas Lobb Chute unfortunately made no effort to improve the situation. A visitor in the 1780s was surprised, even a little shaken, by what he found here.

> 'This noble seat [The Vyne] stands in a soil of deep clay, abounding in wood, which extends northwards over the limits of the County into Berkshire. But those who are travelling hither from Basingstoke, or any southern parts of the county are surprized at the instantaneous change which takes place immediately upon passing from one of those open chalky downs about Basingstoke called Rooksdown, into the deep, low, mirey and wooded village of Sherborne. From thence the road lies up a narrow enclosed lane, which runs across the front of the Vine, into Berkshire; so that some Iron Gates on the left unexpectedly open to the house, which stands a few yards distant from the road, yet protected by a fine, tho' short avenue of trees.'

Such was the inheritance of William John Chute, the thirty-three-year-old eldest son of Thomas Lobb. Older tenants must have remarked on the contrast with his effete kinsman, John Chute. The new squire, brought up in Norfolk, felt himself instantly at home at The Vyne, and never afterwards wished himself to be anywhere else. Far from seeking to improve the landscape, he quickly became a part of it. Superficially a man of taste and refinement, William was at heart a bluff woodlander. For decades to come, he was to manage the estate minimally and reluctantly. Rough and untended, isolated and overgrown, Sherborne at the dawn of the new century was exactly how he liked it.

CHAPTER TWO

William John Chute and the 'Old Régime'

i Pigtails and Trousers

Wis an engaging eccentric who made a powerful impression on his contemporaries. All speak of him as a man out of his time. 'He was a fine specimen of the real old English squire,' wrote one, 'quite one of the old school.' His godson, Wiggett Chute, described how his 'genial and amiable disposition, and general appearance of the polished old English country Gentleman, prepossessed all in his favour, and won all hearts'. According to Edward Austen-Leigh, son of a vicar of Sherborne who had known William all his life, he was 'the very personification of cheerfulness and friendliness. No one ever saw him out of temper, out of patience, or out of spirits. No one ever heard him utter an ill-natured remark, or a coarse expression ... The servant who took undue liberties with him when alive, was miserable at his death; and the agony of grief shown by his brother at his funeral was the most terrible thing of the kind I ever witnessed.' Wiggett Chute's sister Caroline, who lived with him from childhood, summed him up in the words of an old song: 'the very sound of his step upon the stairs was like music in the house'.

It was generally recognised that his manners and attitudes belonged to a lost world. Born in 1757, he had lived for a while in pre-Revolutionary France, and was cheerfully, even obstinately out of step with the new order of things. The most obvious among his idiosyncrasies was his persistence in wearing a pigtail. Long after it had ceased to be fashionable, it hung on by only a few hairs, neatly tied back with a black ribbon. It was a great source of amusement to his much younger brother and heir, Thomas, who referred to it as his 'entailed Propertie'. The pigtail is unfortunately not visible in William's portrait, in middle age, by Emma Smith, though it reveals his hair to have been elaborately curled and powdered.

William and his cousin James Wiggett had been considered great *beaux* during their days together at Cambridge. (They were at Clare Hall, then the smartest of the colleges.) By the time William inherited The Vyne, however, the leaders of fashion were dispensing with dressed hair and wigs and wearing their own hair cut short, though powdered wigs continued, for a while, to be *de rigueur* at court. In 1791, a group of young men left London, rather than face the embarrassment of having to wear them for a Birthday Ball. Four years later, the Tory Prime Minister William Pitt imposed a tax on hair powder (it was made from wheat and considered wasteful in wartime), bringing its widespread use to an immediate end.

Such adornments nevertheless persisted among older men of a conservative bent, an example being Dr Lyford, the Basingstoke surgeon. Edward Austen-Leigh recalled him in the 1860s as 'a fine, tall, old man, with such a flaxen wig as is not to be seen or conceived by this generation'. As an act, supposedly, of charity, Lyford used to donate his used wigs every second year to 'an old man in our parish'. It is presumably Sherborne that is meant (as Lyford had a house there), rather than Steventon, another of his father's livings. In any event, the recipient of Lyford's largesse is said to have been 'as tall and fine looking as himself, producing thereby a ludicrous resemblance between the peasant and the doctor'. Those who clung to these outmoded accessories were apt to make themselves figures of fun. William Chute chose his path when he was still a young man. He continued to wear a pigtail, and to powder his hair, almost to the very end of his long life.

Even more deplorable to him was the transformation, which began in the late eighteenth century, of the gentleman's suit. The trend was away from the gorgeous attire for which that century is famous, with its rich contrasts in colour and material, in favour of dark velvets and silks, an altogether plainer fashion. The shift during the Regency from knee-breeches to trousers was positively traumatic for men like William. A fashionable man about town, Captain Gronow of the Guards, writes that, by 1816, 'knee-breeches were only worn by a few old fogies, trousers and shoes being the usual costume of all the young men of the day'. The Prince Regent himself, shocked at first, soon followed their example; so did William Chute's near neighbour, the Duke of Wellington, though even he was turned away one evening from Almack's Assembly Rooms ('that exclusive temple of the *beau monde*'), whose formidable patronesses remained strictly opposed to the wearing of trousers.

According to James Wiggett's son, William shared with his father 'a great dislike for long loose trousers and black neckcloth, in which we considered ourselves to be dressed, but which he regarded as incorrect and slovenly undress'. Visitors to The Vyne who are shown the splendid silk suit and waistcoats dating from William's youth (found in an attic, they are kept in a chest of drawers in the South Bedroom) may be tempted to sympathise. Gentlemen's suits are as plain and drab today as they can possibly be. Generations of our ancestors knew a gentleman by the colour and quality of his coat. Now, he strives only to be inconspicuous.

Most difficult of all to come to terms with was the increasing familiarity between the sexes. In the early 1800s, it was still the custom for the ladies to lead the way into dinner, the gentlemen following behind. Then it came about that they would walk in together. At first, a gentleman would do no more than touch his partner's hand with the tips of his fingers, but when in time he was expected to proffer his arm, men like William Chute were aghast. He was always, says Wiggett Chute, 'very deferential to the Ladies'.

William had both the courage of his convictions and the freedom to indulge them. His trouser-wearing godson described how they visited a church in London to hear the famous Scottish preacher Irving, at a time when he was attracting large audiences.

'We arrived late, and the Church was as usual crowded, but immediately on our taking a standing position in the aisle, a pew door was opened to him, while I with many others were left standing through the sermon. As he was entering the pew, he turned to me and whispered "See what it is to look like a gentleman".'

ii   Small is beautiful

William's proud, elegant bearing is apparent in the portrait of him attributed to Emma Smith, and it is perhaps not surprising to learn that he was 'exceedingly temperate in his habits'. In an age of gargantuan meals, his breakfast consisted of a few slices of thin bread and butter (which had to be spread by a maid servant, never a man), occasionally a small sausage roll, and a cup of green tea, though always of the very best quality. If he ate rabbit, it had to be wild rather than the home-bred sort; and he would wash it down with a few glasses of 'the best old port'. He held the generally-favoured claret in contempt, declaring that 'his butler old Bush could make as good stuff as that out of the washings of his port wine glasses'.

The old clothes found at The Vyne would have fitted a slender man, who was perhaps about five feet eight inches tall. In view of his spartan diet, it is surprising that William found the energy for so much hard work and exercise. Like all the Chutes, he was motivated by a sense of duty. A natural Tory (the future Prime Minister, Spencer Perceval, had been his fag at Harrow), he represented the County of Hampshire in Parliament for the best part of thirty years. While not afraid on occasion to vote against his party's interest, he never uttered a single word in the House. Edward Austen-Leigh says that he was a poor public speaker and was incapable of making the simplest conversation, though he was no fool and there are ample recorded instances of his quick wit. Indeed, it gave rise to numerous anecdotes.

William is famous not as a reluctant Parliamentarian but as an enthusiastic sportsman, founder of the still-flourishing Vine Hunt (now amalgamated with the Craven). William started a pack of hounds at The Vyne in about 1791, first as harriers, then as fox-hounds. He erected kennels for them in the Office Court that backs onto the kitchen and chapel, now a neat garden. Austen-Leigh describes these tactfully as 'useful rather than ornamental'. Another contemporary calls them 'a miserable hole ... and yet I never saw hounds freer from disease nor able to stand their work *better* than these hounds were'.

Notwithstanding the hideousness of their lodgings, William was devoted to his dogs. He commissioned from his wife, a skilled artist, a little portrait of New Forest Jasper, one of the sires of the pack, and hung it up there. He said the hounds were as entitled as any other great family to have portraits of their ancestors. The picture was inscribed with a witty Latin epigram, and another was painted over the door: 'Multum in parvo'. William seems to have acknowledged that the hounds were small, and that their lodgings were hardly prepossessing: but he knew them to be capable of great things.

His parliamentary duties obliged him to spend much of his time in London, but he would gleefully return to The Vyne at the end of each session, sometimes having his hounds brought out to meet him on the way so that he could have the pleasure of galloping home with them. When in residence, he would order the hounds to be daily paraded before him, for no reason other than for the pleasure of seeing them. The pack normally consisted of about thirty couples, and during the season it would be hunted at least twice and occasionally three times a week. The hunt button was engraved with a vine leaf and tendril and with the initials 'V.H.', though people spoke in those days of 'Mr Chute's hounds' rather than of 'the Vine Hunt'. The membership included most of the local gentry and a preponderance of well-heeled clergymen, as well as a fair representation of the town of Basingstoke (including the younger Charles Lyford, also a surgeon). The clergy element are said to have been a good moral influence on the hunting field, and it was not generally felt - as it was later - that they were in any way corrupted by so rough a distraction.

The meetings, which might take place anywhere between the Kennet and the chalk downs near Winchester, were never advertised. William Chute would turn up

'sitting rather loose on his horse, and his clothes rather loose upon him, the scarlet coat flying open, a little whitened at the collar by the contact of his hair powder and the friction of his pigtail; the frill of his shirt above, and his gold watch-chain and seal below, both rather prominent; the short knee-breeches scarcely meeting the boot tops. See! he rides up, probably with some original amusing remark, at any rate with a cheerful greeting to his friends, a nod and a kindly word to the farmer, and some laughing notice of the schoolboy on his pony.'

Another witness confirms that 'his coat and waistcoat were open, and his shirt fronts got up with broad plaits'. All the men wore round hats, and their scarlet coats were long enough to cover their knees and protect them against the wet or cold.

The smooth running of the hunt was ensured by William's faithful servant, the sharp-eyed Hickson, known to all as George. 'A light, neatly-made man, with a handsome countenance, and a most melodious voice', George is said to have known almost every hound by its bark. He was equipped with a small bugle which he hung from a strap over his shoulder: a more tuneful instrument, apparently, than the traditional straight horn that was carried at the saddle-bow.

George, whose tombstone in the churchyard at Sherborne can still just be read (it is to the right of the porch), was on surprisingly familiar terms with the Master. However, many found him disrespectful and there came a time when he was felt to have got above himself.

Against his better judgement, William was prevailed upon to dismiss him and to take on a huntsman from Norfolk called Cane. William found him unsatisfactory, and gleefully reinstated the faithful George. As his brother Thomas Chute, a shameless if erudite punster, put it, he was heartily relieved to find himself 'cum canibus, sine Cane' *(still with his dogs, but without Cane)*.

Tom Chute was remembered as 'a better sportsman, and a far bolder rider,' than his brother. William preferred to dismount and lead his horse over obstacles, even imaginery ones. At other times he would catch hold of its tail and allow himself to be pulled over. As he was dismounting on one occasion, he told a farmer who was with him that he would lead his horse over the ditch. 'But there is no ditch,' said the farmer, 'and your horse will walk over.' 'But I fancy there is a ditch,' William replied, 'and that is the same thing.'

On another long run, from Sherborne to Chawton, William dismounted at a fence out of Bradley Wood.

'He slipped as he was leading his horse, and the animal trod heavily on his thigh. Those who were near were in great alarm, but he got up with no other injury than a bruise. Mr John Portal expressed his delight that it was no worse, saying, "I thought we were going to lose our member." "Did you?" he replied, rubbing the injured part. "Well, I can tell you I thought I was going to lose mine."'

iii   A Gallic shrug

Everyone in this area must have had a favourite story to tell about William Chute, but most are unrecorded. William was in Basingstoke one day, settling his coal bill. He complained to his supplier that the prices were excessive. 'Well sir,' the man replied, 'you must remember that coals *is* coals, in these times.' 'Indeed,' said William, 'I am glad to hear you say so; for what you have sent me lately have been mostly slates.'

As one would expect, he kept a very merry house. William spoke excellent French, having lived at Angers for a while after Cambridge. He used to give a convincing impersonation of a Frenchman, complete with the appropriate shrugs and grimaces. A regular visitor was his brother Tom. 'The jokes that passed between them and the amusing differences of opinion on relative distances to particular places, and in hunting matters among other things formed quite a comedy.' The pair were devoted to each other. (A middle brother, Chaloner, had died at The Vyne in February 1790, 'of a fever occasioned by his exertions while canvassing for his brother at the General Election'.) Tom, who lived at Pickenham, referred to William as his 'dear Bro'.

William had been married since 1793 to Elizabeth or 'Eliza', daughter of Joshua Smith of Earle Stoke in Wiltshire, the Member of Parliament for Devizes. An intelligent and unassuming woman, who enjoyed novels and painting, she appears from her diaries to have led a quiet and rather lonely life, especially as the ladies excluded themselves from the hunt. She had to resign herself, moreover, to what must have been a great sorrow in her life: her childlessness. A solution was found in 1803, when James Wiggett presented his eldest daughter Caroline to the couple as a sort of pet. The child was only three years old and had lost her own mother. Infants of good family were often farmed out to strangers, and Wiggett must have thought he was doing his best by her. The experience was nevertheless deeply distressing for Caroline:

'I believe the following summer of my arrival at the Vyne my Father came to see me, but I remember crying when he took me on his knee, but showing me his watch soon pacified me ... For many years after I seldom heard of my own family, and still less saw them.'

Indeed, she was about twelve years old when she was next, briefly reunited with them, at Bath; and nearly sixty years after that, it pained her to recall that her youngest sister had had to ask who she was. Caroline's consolation was the kindness she received at The Vyne. She was on excellent terms with her good-natured, humorous uncles, William and Thomas, and the 'old women of the village called me a pretty little dear'. Only with 'Aunt Chute' and her relations was she ill at ease. Though they were 'very kind to me, I ever felt I did not belong to them,' she writes.

Amongst the incidents of her happy childhood, Caroline recalls how the occasional dinner party

'made quite a stir in the house, and was looked forward to by the whole household with the greatest pleasure, to see the *gentlefolks* come out of their carriages, the bringing out of the sweet things, and the *really* good plate, and to be dressed in my best white frock and pink sash, they were simple, happy days.'

Dinner was taken much earlier then, at about half past three in the afternoon. Any children present would therefore be allowed into the dining room (the Saloon of today) for the dessert - 'unencumbered,' as she points out,

'with flounces and crinolines, or the long hair as in these days, a little plain frock, with a tuck or two, and the hair cut short like a boy's, I never wore a curl till I was 15. Uncle Thomas would have cut them off if he had seen them, the style of dress was so simple then.'

Another favourite spectacle was the hunt assembling at the house:

'A very great excitement to see the gentlemen in their red coats, to hear the horn blow, and George's (the huntman's) melodious voice calling his hounds ... nothing daunted at the hearing of the bugle, out I was, over the hedges and ditch tally hoing at the top of my voice ...'

iv   Horses for dinner

The house must have seemed to awaken at such moments from a deep sleep, but for an imaginative child it was, at all times, a place of enchantment. Ivy-clad and surrounded by long grass, it seems then to have been screened from the road by 'quantities of ancient trees', so one came upon it unexpectedly. The entrance was on the side of the stable block: John Webb's stone piers and the iron gates were moved to their present position in 1911, when Sir Charles Chute created the new drive which leads directly to the house. There was already an avenue, though, formed of decaying elms which are supposed to have been planted by the Speaker himself. The main gates opened onto a narrow gravel drive which led, past the stables and brewhouse, down to the front entrance, passing on the right hand side a 'large old basin, with a hedge row of fine chestnut trees before it, and laurels inter-mixed making a sort of shrubbery'. Behind the basin, on a lower level, were the kennels and their noisy occupants. The house itself appeared to nestle in a sort of hollow, and was indeed on a lower level than the ground in front of it, which was subsequently reduced by as much as six feet. Beyond the balustrade (also since lowered), with its two stone eagles that had been the gift of Horace Walpole - their heads and wings more than a little worn by now - a couple of steps led down to the front door. The porch, the gable on the central tower and the bay-windows on the end of each wing were added by a later owner.

The ground on the other side between the house and the water was far from being the immaculate lawn that it is today. Never mown, it was used as pasture for William's hunters, a purpose for which it was well suited. One of the excitements of dinner at The Vyne (in what is now the Saloon, then painted bright blue) was that the inquisitive hunters often used to poke their heads through the open windows. They are said to have grown so fat over the summer that it took them half the season to get fit. William dedicated all his resources to the hounds and his horses were of distinctly inferior quality, unlike the race-horses that had been bred here by an earlier generation of the family. In 1688, Edward Chute had won a magnificent silver punch-bowl at the Basingstoke Races, run on the downs to the west of the town, and the portrait of him (formerly thought to be of his son Anthony) has a race-horse and jockey in the background. The association with Basingstoke Races was kept up by William, whose huntsman and whipper-in used to clear the course, cutting a fine figure in their scarlet coats. George's preferred mount on these occasions was a bad-tempered animal called 'The Kicker', because he reacted adversely to being touched on the rump. If George 'found the mob inclined to close in again too soon after he had passed along the ropes, he just touched The Kicker on the rump, who immediately justi-fied his name, and compelled the crowd to keep their distance'. The site of the old course - on the east side of Kempshott Lane, south of what used to be Buckskin Farm - is now, inevitably, a forest of *bijou* dwellings.

William's want of money to spend on horses was a consequence of his wilful mismanagement of the estate, which, as Austen-Leigh puts it, 'was singularly capable of improvement'.

> 'Its clay soil and small enclosures were overrun with oak timber; it required clearing like an American forest, draining like an Irish bog. In those days oak timber was of great value; and he might have cut many thousands of pounds' worth of it, and have increased the annual rents of his estate by doing so. But he never could bring himself to make any change ... By him no hedgerow was grubbed, no sunshine let in upon his woodland fields, no land drained, no roads improved. His delight was to keep everything exactly as he had found it'

Many people must have thought him downright peculiar. Not only did he revel in decay, but he seems to have lacked any appreciation of the artistic treasures in his house. The chapel was never opened up, except to be shown to the occasional stranger. The Oak Gallery doubled as Caroline's play-room and as a store for lumber, its glories wholly unappreciated. Visitors who asked to see the 'picture gallery' would be shown the majestic grove of oaks in front of the house instead of the Dutch landscapes and Poussins. As for Morgaston Wood, it was all but impenetrable, apart from a single path which cut through it as far as Pollards' End. Caroline says that her uncle could not bear to cut anything down. He famously refused a large sum for the mighty oak which stands beside the Summer House, the so-called 'Hundred Guinea' or 'Grand Piano' oak. Two hundred years ago, the tree was separated from the road by a ditch, not fenced in as it is today. A passing timber merchant (an Admiralty agent, according to one account) offered William a hundred pounds for it, which were refused. The next day the man returned, this time offering a hundred *guineas*. Even this was refused. If his oaks grew five pounds a night in value, William explained, then he ought to hang on to them a little longer.

He was inclined to turn down any and every opportunity for enrichment almost as a matter of principle. It is no surprise that the home farm, Vyne Lodge Farm, was an unprofitable venture. Cox, for many years the bailiff, was amiable but incompetent. According to Austen-Leigh, William

> 'took an actual pleasure in this man's failures, and was most especially delighted whenever the hay intended for farm purposes was injured, after he had secured all that he required for his hunters in good condition. I once expressed to him my concern at having seen his hay out in the rain. "My hay!" said he; "what do you mean? I've no hay out; I got all mine up famously last week." I mentioned to him the name of the field in which I had observed it. "Oh pooh!" said he, "that was not my hay, that was Coxe's. Silly fellow, it serves him right, and I am glad of it; he might have got it all up a week ago if he had had any sense."'

v   Ridge and Furrow

The productivity of other parts of the estate, which were held on half-yearly tenure by various small occupiers, was of even less concern to William. Needless to say, these lands had been unreformed since the Middle Ages. South of the village, on either side of the Aldermaston Road, were the open fields, where all the villagers worked together to produce a common crop. The scene was unchanged in any particular since the days when Henry III had passed through on his way to Sherborne Priory, or the Lord of Saint John had ridden out to Gascony, after paying his respects at the tombs of his ancestors. The so-called 'Middle' and 'Upper' fields, which were cultivated right up to the edge of Crane's Road, were divided into scores of irregular strips, some of them smaller, some greater than an acre. The village plough team, traditionally of eight oxen (more than any individual tenant could muster), would snake up and down each strip, creating a central ridge-and-furrow, like an inverted S, that was particularly distinctive in heavy clay. The headlands at either end, on which the plough team would turn, were left as grassy banks. Each tenant would hold a distribution of these small strips which was scattered across various parts of the common land, some holdings being more considerable than others.

In the time of William John Chute, the movement towards enclosure was slow but inexorable. His estate was classically in need of such reform. After the harvest, when others were planting winter crops, the Sherborne peasantry let their cattle loose in the open fields. Their winter produce consisted not of turnips and swede, but of thistles and weeds. Their woodland holdings, which might have been better used, were an almost worthless collection of damp, sunless enclosures, each bounded by wide oak and hazel rows. Rooksdown, at the south-western extremity of the parish, was but a poor pasture, all gorse and heath, and unfenced. The Moor, delimited on the north side by the Weybrook where it flows through Morgaston Wood, was the common meadow, divided into strips for the production of a hay crop, but was then and is still half covered by water after heavy rain. The tenants themselves lacked both the resources and the initiative for change. Some of them lived elsewhere, particularly at Basingstoke, as in many cases there was no house attached to their holding. Very few had any capital and many, unsurprisingly, were in almost permanent arrears with their rent. Sherborne in the early 1800s, like its fustian and eccentric squire, was firmly locked in the past.

CHAPTER THREE

The Fine Retreat

i Ends and Greens

Its medieval lords had driven back the boundaries of Pamber Forest and had created the common fields for their serfs, but Sherborne continued for centuries to be the collection of inhabited woodland clearings that it had been since ancient times. West End and Church End are still thought of as separate entities, but Mill End (the settlement at the end of Mill Lane, around the former Mill) has been depopulated within living memory. The existence of Vyne Green has been entirely forgotten. As for Smith's Green, now a cluster of nine-teenth-century cottages, only its name and some medieval finds in the nearby fields give any clue to its being an abandoned hamlet.

Other settlements had flourished alongside the Roman road which linked Venta Belgarum (Winchester) and nearby Calleva Atrebatum (Silchester), an important regional capital both before and during the Roman period. A small part of the Aldermaston Road, south of the village (roughly, that is, between Gale's Garage and Dixon's Corner), still follows the course of the old road. Otherwise it was gradually abandoned in the Middle Ages, after the invading Saxons had turned Calleva into a ghost town. Medieval traffic was diverted instead through West End and onwards in the direction of Aldermaston, along a road which is now insanely busy, but which for many centuries was an insignificant thoroughfare. It was called the Aldermaston Road (though it fetched up eventually in the centre of Reading) because that was the first village of any size through which it passed: the country in between was but thinly populated. The Cavalier Colonel Gage had found Aldermaston a convenient hiding-place in 1644, it being, as he put it, 'a village out of any great road'.

Travellers by this route used to come almost immediately upon Story's, or Sherborne Green, on the north side of West End. As a separate hamlet, it had perhaps never amounted to more than the two or three cottages which were there in Anthony Chute's time (mid-eighteenth century), and which are still marked on the Tithe map of 1840. The green had been created in a fork between the Aldermaston Road and a trackway which led off to the north-east, across the fields and into Morgaston Wood. The trackway soon merged with the old Roman Road and was known as Pollard's End Lane. Another road of sorts, of which there is no longer any trace, linked Story's Green with Mill End. There was also a 'Trotway', mentioned in 1771, which peeled south from here to emerge at the Vicarage.

The lane which led into Morgaston Wood, and ultimately to Bramley, took its name from yet another lost hamlet which stood at what is now the southern edge of the Wood. First documented in 1313, Pollard's End had been reduced by 1842 from four to a mere three cottages, and was soon to disappear altogether. The platforms for the cottages and a pond are all that remains.

Beyond Pollard's End, the once mighty Roman road continued its dead straight course through the Wood, and at this point its two outer banks and inner ditches, together with the *agger* of the road itself, are still discernible to the expert eye. North of the Wood (the boundary of which has been marked since the 1830s by Morgaston Road), it long remained a public highway, though much reduced in scale. It was not until 1414, a full thousand years after the withdrawal of the legions, that William Brocas had been licensed finally to close off that part of it that had crossed his park at Beaurepaire, on condition that he create an alternative route of equivalent length and breadth. Thenceforth, the medieval lane that had followed its course suddenly veered off in a north-easterly direction, whilst a track branching off to the left, known as Peat Gully Road, eventually came out on the Pamber Road, both routes conveniently by-passing Brocas's park. Peat Gully Road was also the way to Hill End, Sherborne's outermost settlement, of which there is record from the early fifteenth century. A small community still exists around Hillend Farm, though access today is from the Aldermaston Road, at Salter's Heath. Those bound for Beaurepaire or Bramley, however, kept to the now forgotten lane (which Wiggett Chute calls 'impassable'), of which only a small stretch, between Beaurepaire Farm and House, has been preserved.

The roads had in no way improved since the time when Horace Walpole mounted his summer expeditions to The Vyne. They 'had ruts deep enough to bury *me* in,' writes Caroline Wiggett, 'and they were rendered worse by the trees overhanging them.' Wiggett Chute describes them as 'little better than driftways, and generally impassable to anything but carts or waggons'. Wheeled traffic might make it as far as the gates of The Vyne, but would need to find an alternative route to Bramley. Between the walled garden and the car park, there is still the opening to a track that led to the lodge gate of Beaurepaire Park. Another option was to go up to the Home Farm, and thence, by a dirt track, to Cufaude Lane. A rare initiative on the part of William John Chute was his creation, in about 1808, of a new gravel drive between the house and the farm. It was about all he could manage on his limited resources. The present straight road to Bramley, built by Wiggett Chute in 1845, was a more obvious improvement.

The Aldermaston Road is the only local road that was regularly maintained: it was turnpiked, with a toll gate at Pamber End. Others were mere 'green lanes', some of them, to a modern eye, looking more like bridleways, hardly deserving to be called roads at all. Two hundred years ago, all roads and ways were much the same. When the lanes were muddy, which was most of the time, they were impenetrable to any woman who cared about her appearance. In *Pride and Prejudice,* Elizabeth Bennett creates astonishment when she calls on the Bingley household 'with weary ankles, dirty stockings, and a face glowing with exercise ... That she should have walked three miles so early in the day, in such dirty weather and by herself, was almost incredible to Mrs Hurst and Miss Bingley; and Elizabeth was convinced that they held her in contempt for it'. It was usual even for gentlewomen (including Jane Austen, no slave in any case to fashion) to hook under their shoes a pair of raised wooden soles or *pattens* in order to get about. It was a small price to pay for one's independence.

Most people had no means of transport other than their feet. As William Clift of Bramley (born in 1828) recalls in his memoirs, 'foot people walked inside the fields on the footpaths, it being impossible for them to get along the lanes, in which only strong carts and waggons could be used'. They would of course think nothing of walking the two miles from Sherborne to Basingstoke, a hazardous, if not an impossible undertaking today. An eighty-eight-year-old Bramley woman recalled to Clift in 1908 how she had once walked in her pattens to Maidenhead (over twenty miles) in a single day. Unfortunately, with numerous fords to be negotiated hereabouts, it might have been difficult to keep one's feet dry.

The Chute household was one of the few which enjoyed the blessing of a carriage. It put them within relatively easy reach of London (five and a half hours on a good day, including a twenty-minute stop at Bagshot). The family took walks for pleasure, but only in the summer-time. They liked going into Morgaston Wood to hear the nightingales. At other times they would walk to Bramley or to Beaurepaire, which no one would attempt to reach 'except on horse back or foot'. The north part of the parish was considered so inaccessible that there was a saying locally: 'The Vyne is the last place on earth, and Beaurepaire is beyond it'. Secluded from the world, the Beaurepaire estate was deeply romantic and mysterious. Caroline recalls that it

'was a mile but untenanted except once in two or three years [when] an old-fashioned Mrs Brocas, step-grandmother to the later Mr Brocas, came for a couple of months, in a large coach drawn by four black long-tailed horses, required I am sure to get her through the ruts ... It was a great treat to walk there and see the curious old lady, and the moat with which the house was surrounded. The village of Bramley, a mile further, sometimes we walked to, to see the handsome monument there of old Mrs Brocas supporting her dying husband. The ruts were so deep and the paths so dirty these excursions were only taken in the summer, all the trees around as thick as the wood itself ...'

At one time, not so long ago, Beaurepaire had been a gay and busy place. Bernard Brocas had served dutifully as a magistrate and as Lieutenant-Colonel of the North Hants Militia, and his interests had extended across the border into Berkshire. The family estates (including a farm that is still called 'Brocas Land' at Mortimer), had stretched from Burghfield Hill to Basingstoke. Harriot Brocas, daughter to John Lannoy Hunter of Beech Hill, was Bernard's second wife, whom he had married in 1769. Unfortunately, neither she nor his first wife (a Miss Reeve of Arborfield) had borne him children. The heir was his natural son, Bernard Austin, born in London in 1765, whom he had formally adopted at the age of nine, no doubt with Harriot's full approval. Young Bernard had not only been given his father's surname, but had been prepared for his inheritance with an education at Harrow and Cambridge, whence he had been duly commissioned into the Berkshire Militia.

During their brief years together, the Brocases had divided their time between Beaurepaire and another seat, Wokefield Park, a mere five miles away at Stratfield Mortimer. Their heavy household goods would be carted from one house to the other in due season. After the elder Bernard's death in 1777, aged 47, the widowed Harriot, who lived until 1819, had increasingly favoured Wokefield as a residence, for according to William Clift,

> 'when she wanted to go from one house to the other, the journey took her the best part of a day to do it; and I've been told that she used to drive four black horses, and then could only go at foot pace, with two men walking by the side carrying poles with which they could help the wheels out of the deep ruts from time to time.'

ii   The Pride of the Gascon

The mansion at Beaurepaire was enormous: a show of grandeur that was intended, one suspects, to be taken notice of at the neighbouring Vyne. Though contained by a medieval moat, it was a modern house, built by the late Mr Brocas himself. Having come of age in 1751, a year after the death of his father, he had initially forsaken the ancestral home in favour of Wokefield (itself to be rebuilt in the nineteenth century), which he had bought from the Earl of Uxbridge. The old house at Beaurepaire had been demolished by 1758, when Bernard refers to it as his 'late house'. It had soon been resurrected, though, as an imposing and oversized folly, its diapered brickwork exactly matching that at The Vyne. A clumsy, three-storeyed building, it had battlements, corner towers, and even a spire, topped by a weather vane. The artificial lake in the park, intended for use as a skating rink, and known, curiously, as 'Westminster Pond', was not one of Mr Brocas's indulgences, as it dates from the turn of the twentieth century, but perhaps he would have skated on the medieval stews (which still exist), like some figure painted by Raeburn or Gilbert Stuart.

There is unfortunately little record of the previous building on the site, which dated from the reign of Henry III. Beaurepaire had begun as another of Sherborne's sub-manors, created by William de Saint John out of his vast holding, and granted to a retainer, Bartholomew Pecche, in return for his homage and services. The impoverished Pecches had sold out in 1353, to Master Bernard de Brocas, a Gascon cleric. The wealthy Rector of St

Nicholas, Guildford, Master Bernard had paid a hundred silver marks for the dilapidated manor-house and for the small, run-down estate that surrounded it.

The Brocas family were devoted servants of the Plantagenet kings, the lords of their native Gascony. Arnald de Brocas had fallen at Bannockburn: a grateful Edward II had generously provided for his sons, who included Bernard, by overseeing their education. When of age, he had appointed them to a variety of official positions. The eldest boy, John, eventually became Constable of Guildford for Edward III. He was knighted in 1340, perhaps after distinguishing himself at the great sea-battle off Sluys. John had been the first of the family to acquire property in Hampshire, receiving, in 1338, the grant of some lands in Basingstoke. As a celibate priest, Bernard must always have intended Beaurepaire for John's son, another Bernard, to whom, after a couple of years, he had made it over. Young Bernard, boyhood companion and squire to the Black Prince, had probably fought at Crecy and had himself been knighted by 1354. The deed of transfer is dated 9 July 1356. Within weeks, Sir Bernard was in action again at Poitiers, where he witnessed the capture (by Bernard du Troy) of the French king. The victory was marked at home by solemn services of thanksgiving in the churches, and by the lighting of bonfires in every town and village. These were events in which the people of Sherborne St John may have taken particular pride.

Sir Bernard fully intended to settle at Beaurepaire, and was soon committing large sums to its restoration. The main building, consisting of a hall, chambers and a kitchen, was completely re-roofed (the tiles came from Odiham), as were the chapel and grange. New doors were sawn, two new ovens installed in the kitchen, and hearths made in three of the chambers. The chapel was fitted with a glass window, an expensive luxury at the time, and all the internal walls were plastered over 'with the lord's lime'. The estate was poorly fenced, so a hedge was made, at great cost, 'in different places about the lands and meadows'. With the King's permission, Sir Bernard enclosed the deer-park in 1369 and enlarged it in 1388, at the expense of the ever-receding Forest of Pamber. For a while, at least, the family was obliged to put up with the Roman road that ran so inconveniently through its midst.*

Sir Bernard Brocas, described by a French chronicler as a 'tres bon chevalier', was Constable of Aquitaine for a couple of years from 1364, fought beside the Black Prince at Najara, and crowned his career, in 1377, with the Captaincy of Calais (the most coveted of military appointments, and one which was later held by another Sherborne resident, the

---

*Another acquisition in this period was the small estate in Sherborne St John called 'le Cranys', bought by Oliver Brocas, Sir Bernard's much younger half-brother, in 1396. The vendor, Thomas Munde, was a citizen and goldsmith of London, whose mother-in-law, Elizabeth Everard, had previously resided there. Oliver was to live out his days in the main house, 'Cranysplace', on the corner of the Aldermaston Road and Crane's Road, and to die at a great age in about 1437. (The present Crane's Farmhouse is an old timber-framed building. It has yet to be ascertained whether any part of it dates from Oliver's time. The frame, largely concealed by later rendering and extensions, is still exposed on the western gable.) Later combined with Beaurepaire, and leased out to tenants, Crane's was treated, for historical reasons, as a separate manor. The minutes of its own manorial courts survive from as recently as 1614. In the nineteenth century, it finally passed from Brocas hands into those of Wiggett Chute. With it went 'a very small piece' of land on the opposite side of Crane's Road (now part of a greater field), described in 1476 as 'the gret orchard afor the yat [gate] of the said messuage [house]'.

first Lord Sandys). Sir Bernard's second marriage (after 1381) to Mary, daughter and heiress of Sir John des Roches, entitled him, moreover, to claim a colourful and lucrative office, the Mastership of the Royal Buckhounds. It was attached to the lordship of Hunter's Manor in Little Weldon, Northamptonshire, near Rockingham Castle, which was a favourite royal residence and hunting retreat. Little Weldon had been Mary's inheritance from her first husband, Sir John de Borhunte, but Sir Bernard ensured that with royal consent the Mastership would remain with himself and his heirs, for as long as they retained Little Weldon. His descendants clung on to both the office and the manor until their sale - a sad day for the Brocases - in 1633. (The Dymokes of Scrivelsby in Lincolnshire have been more tenacious, and still hold the office of the Honourable the Queen's Champion, in which capacity their representative attended the Coronation of Elizabeth II in 1953.)

Sir Bernard died in 1395. A mark of his distinction, and the esteem of his King, is that he was splendidly buried in Westminster Abbey, amongst all the royal tombs in St Edmund's Chapel. His local church was not forgotten, though: by a handsome bequest of forty marks, he is thought to have endowed the Brocas Chapel at St Andrew's. This was erected on the north side of the chancel, was the burial-place of generations of Sir Bernard's descendants, and is adorned with a fine collection of monumental brasses. There is a later Bernard on his knees, in armour and heraldic surcoat, above a grisly *memento mori,* the skeleton of a king, whose crown is useless to him now. There is John flanked by his two wives, one the mother of six children and the other of five, who are depicted beneath their respective parents, as if queuing up to pray. William, too, is shown in the traditional pose, but there are words issuing from his mouth on a scroll: 'O Blessed Trinite have mercy on me'.

More prominent than the brasses is the impressive sarcophagus that divides the chapel from the chancel. It commemorates Edith, heiress to the senior Brocas line, who died in 1517, and her husband, Ralph Pexall. On top are the life-size effigies of the couple. Ralph is clad in the armour that he would never have worn in life: he was a royal clerk by profession. Edith wears a 'kennel' headdress and hairnet, a pleated chemise and a low-cut bodice. Each figure at one time carried a heart, but these have broken away. Sir Richard Pexall, the couple's son, succeeded to Beaurepaire and to the Mastership of the Royal Buckhounds. He contracted an advantageous first marriage to Lady Elinor Paulet, daughter of the first Marquess of Winchester (who turned Basing into the grandest private house in England); and a second, childless one, to Elinor Cotgrave. Once commended by Queen Mary for his 'good, true and faithful service', Sir Richard was buried in 1571 in Westminster Abbey, close to the tomb of Sir Bernard; but the Pexall reign ended with him, for the marriage of Anne, his youngest daughter and heiress, to Bernard Brocas of Horton in Buckinghamshire (they were fifth cousins) was to restore the surviving male line of the Brocas family to its ancestral property.

Unsophisticated as it may now have seemed in comparison to The Vyne, Beaurepaire was nevertheless deemed worthy of the occasional royal visit. Henry VIII had spent a couple of days there in August 1531, as Ralph Pexall's guest; enjoying the hunting, no doubt, as he paid 'to the Keeper of Baroper Park in rewarde, VIs. VIIId.' A day later, he gives a further twenty shillings 'to a servant of Pexall in rewarde at Baroper Park'. Scornful of the quaint, though serviceable thirteenth-century manor-house, and in no position to remodel it in emulation of Lord Sandys, Sir Richard Pexall had turned it into a dower-house and decamped to nearby Steventon, whose manor-house he rebuilt. Sir Richard's widow, Dame Elinor, who was duly installed at Beaurepaire, was to import a further three husbands in succession. Among them was Sir John Savage, a notorious figure in family legend, who was bent on usurping both the estate and the Mastership for the benefit of himself and his son. Only after the death of Dame Elinor, in 1617 or 18, did the Brocases have any prospect of returning to Beaurepaire.

iii   Elizabeth I Slept Here

It was during the Savage ascendancy, in September 1601, that the house had been visited by Queen Elizabeth I. Nothing is known of her stay, except that it was marked in Bramley by a peal of bells: the fee paid to the bellringers is entered in the parish register. The Queen had progressed since mid-August from Windsor to Caversham, and had then pitched up, with barely any warning, at Basing House. As the harrassed clerk of its kitchen wrote to a friend, 'all things for so great entertainment but elbow room and good will were wanting'. Whilst the Lord Winchester was ruinously providing for the royal household at his own expense, Elizabeth planned to accommodate additional guests at The Vyne. A special embassy from France, under the Duc de Gontaut-Biron, was newly arrived in London. The ducal train (including twenty-seven noblemen) amounted to nearly four hundred persons, more than even Basing could absorb. However, the Lord Sandys of The Vyne, a supporter of the recent Essex rebellion, had been dispossessed (if only temporarily), and his furniture cleared out. On 29 August, Elizabeth had sent instructions to her Council in London. The Earl of Cumberland was to escort the Frenchmen to The Vyne, but first was to lay on 'a solemn reception' in the capital, which would allow her time to refurbish the vacant house.

Lord Cumberland seems to have performed his duties with a poor grace and little vigour. When Sir Walter Ralegh introduced himself to the French party about a week later, he discovered that they had neither seen nor heard from him in days. Himself a fluent French speaker (as a young man he had fought for the Protestant cause in Brittany), Ralegh had taken it upon himself to conduct a sight-seeing tour. He took them

'to Westminster to see the monuments; and this Monnday we entertayned them at the Bear Garden [an arena for bear-baiting, on the Bankside at Southwark], which they had great pleasure to see. Here hathe been with them Sir A. Savage and Sir Arthur Gorges, who hathe bynn their guides, - without whom they had byn left allone. Their horses will not be provided till Wensday morninge. The posts say they cannot take up horses without cummission from the Lords of the Concell. I sent to and fro, and have labored like a moyle [mule] to fashion things so as on Wensday night they wilbe att Bagshoot, and Thursday at the Vine.'

The arrival of the French in Sherborne must have been a momentous event in the locality, remembered and talked about for years. On 9 September, the Queen had commanded the Sheriff of Hampshire 'to attend the Duke of Biron at his coming into that country'. On 10 September he had set out on the London road and had met the cavalcade at Blackwater. He had conducted them that same evening to The Vyne. According to John Stow, the London historian, it had been hastily furnished

> 'with hangings and plate from the Tower and Hampton Court, and with seven score beds and furniture, which the willing and obedient people of Hampshire upon two days' warning had brought thither to lend to the Queen'.

Among those who loaned furniture were probably the heads of the Kingsmill, Tichborne and Hungerford families, soon to be knighted by the Queen. Savage of Beaurepaire may also have played a part, to ensure that the four hundred or so Frenchmen had at least a hundred and forty beds between them. Each bed could have accommodated several people, but most of the party would have bedded down on the floor, and thought nothing of it. The state rooms in such houses routinely doubled as dormitories. Chief among them was the 'great dynyng chamber', thought to be the Saloon of today, though it was still in use as a dining-room in the time of William John Chute. When William inherited, the fine oak panelling in this room was covered with blue paint. According to a description from 1780, it was 'of a vast length, is painted dark blue, small old panels, in each of which is a gold star, the cornice gilt'. The 'starry sky' effect had been in vogue since the Middle Ages, and the *décor* here is unlikely to have changed since the Tudor period. If indeed this was the 'great dynyng chamber', it had contained in 1541 a trestle table that was five yards long, a dais, a 'cupboard' for the display of plate, nine 'hangings of imagery', a 'large fyne carpet', and satin curtains. There had been a single chair, covered in black velvet, trimmed with gold, but also dozens of cushions, sumptuously covered, for the comfort of those resorting to the floor. Had any of these essential ingredients been missing, Elizabeth would have organised replacements. Thus assured of dignified accommodation, the Frenchmen were happily entertained for four or five days, 'all at the Queen's charges'.

To Ralegh's distress, the foreigners wore 'all black and no kind of bravery at all': were they in mourning? Famous (even among the French) for the magnificence of his wardrobe, he had tactfully left behind all his usual suits and had had his tailor run one up in black taffeta. His own taste (to judge from his portraits) was for silver satin doublets, studded with pearls, for great wheel-ruffs edged with lace, for plush cloaks lined with fur, and for jewel-encrusted bonnets in the style of *Henri Trois*. After only two days in Hampshire, Ralegh rode back to London by night (promising to return to Basing within three days) for the express purpose of seeing his tailor and saddler. The one was to supply him with a 'playne taffeta sute' and the other with a 'playne black saddell'. It clearly grieved him at any time to be inappropriately dressed.

Biron was a Marshal of France, and his King's favourite. Though his mission was to discuss foreign affairs with Elizabeth, she was determined to impress upon him the superiority of her court. The magnificence of her nobility, 'so costly furnished and mounted', was shown off at their first meeting, when they hunted together at Basing. Their next encounter, at The Vyne, is described by Stow:

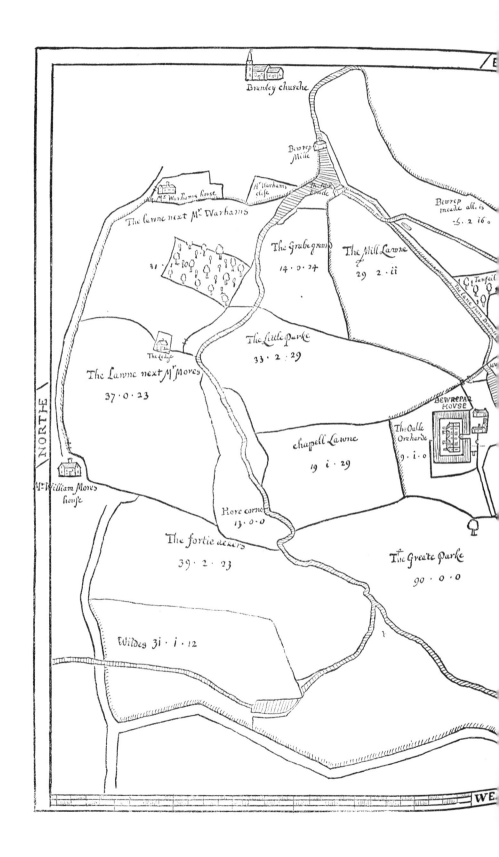

Brumley churche

Bewrep Mille

Mr Warhams close

Mr Warhams house

The Milk Ponde

Bewrep meade all is -5. 2. 16 0

The lawne next Mr Warhams

The Grabe grownd 14 · 0 · 24

The Mill Lawne 29 2 · ii

31 ·

Tanfeil the lane from Brom

The Lodge

The Lawne next Mr Mores 37 · 0 · 23

The Little parke 33 · 2 : 29

We

BEWREPAR HOVSE

The Oulde Orcharde 9 · i · 0

Mr William Mores house

chapell Lawne 19 i · 29

Hore corner 13 · 0 · 0

The fortie ackers 39 · 2 · 23

The Greete parke 90 · 0 · 0

Wildes 3i · i · 12

NORTHE

E

WE

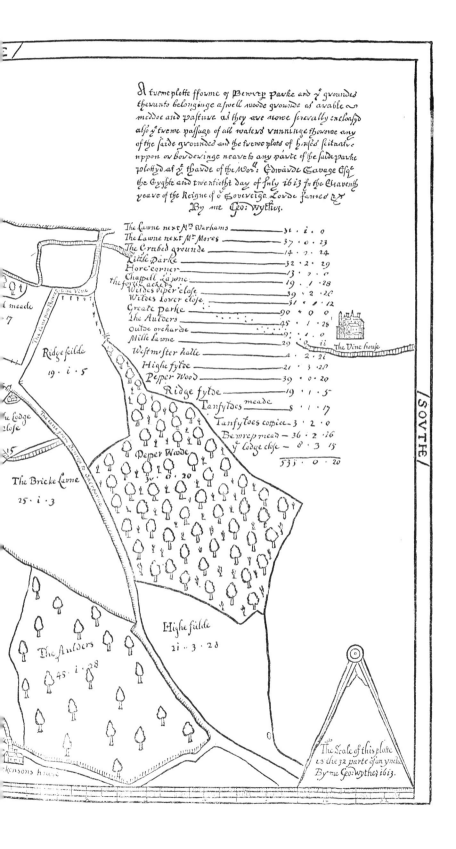

A trewe plotte fforme of Bewrep parke and ye grounded therunto belonginge aswell woode grounde as arable meddoe and pasture as they are nowe severally encloasyd also ye trewe passage of all waters runninge thorowe any of the saide grounded and the trewe plots of housed scituate uppon or bordewinge neare to any parte of the saide parke plotfyd at ye thande of the Worll Edwarde Savage Esqr the Eyghte and twentieth day of July 1613 in the eleaventh yeare of the Reigne of o Sovereigne Lorde James &c.
By me Geo: Wytliers.

The Lawne next Mr Warhams ——————— 31 . 1 . 0
The Lawne next Mr Mores ——————— 37 . 0 . 23
The Crubed grounde ——————— 14 . 2 . 14
Little Parke ——————— 32 . 2 . 29
Hore corner ——————— 13 . 2 . 0
Chappell Lawne ——————— 19 . 1 . 28
The forte ackers ——————— 39 . 2 . 20
Wildes viper close ——————— 31 . 1 . 12
Wildes lower close ——————— 90 . 0 . 0
Greate parke ——————— 45 . 1 . 28
The Aulders ——————— 9 . 1 . 0
Oulde orcharde ——————— 29 . 0 . 11
Mille Lawne ——————— The Vine house
Wistmester halle ——————— 4 . 2 . 21
Highe fylde ——————— 21 . 3 . 20
Pepper Wood ——————— 39 . 0 . 20
Ridge fylde ——————— 19 . 1 . 5
Tanfyldes meade ——————— 8 . 1 . 17
Tanfytoes coppice — 3 . 2 . 0
Bewrep mead — 36 . 2 . 16
ye Lodge close — 8 . 3 . 15
                                535 . 0 . 20

Ridge feilde
19 . 1 . 5

The lodge close

The Bricke Lawne
25 . 1 . 3

Pepper Woode
31 . 0 . 20

The Aulders
45 . 1 . 28

Highe fiilde
21 . 3 . 28

SOVTHE

kensons house

The Scale of this plotte
is the 32 parte of an ynch
By me Geo: wyther 1613.

'when she came to the place where the Duke stayed, the said Sheriff (as the manner is), bare-headed and riding next before her, stayed his horse, thinking the Queen would then have saluted the Duke; whereat the Queen being much offended, commanded the Sheriff to go on. The Duke followed her very humbly, bowing low towards her horse's mane, with his cap off, about two hundred yards. Her Majesty on the sudden took off her mask, looked back upon him, and most graciously and courteously saluted him; as if holding it not becoming so mighty a prince as she was, and who so well knew all kingly majesty, to make her stay directly upon a subject, before he had showed his obedience in following after her.'

The handsome Biron was far from being overwhelmed or intimidated by his reception. According to a French source, Sully, he applied his own considerable charm and was soon able to converse freely with the Queen. He even dared to express his sympathy for the Earl of Essex, the former favourite whom she had recently executed. In reply, the Queen told him that she wished it had been otherwise, but Essex had refused to submit to her, despite the incontestable proof of his treason. As the Queen herself must have observed, Biron was the French Essex. Already plotting treason against his King, he, too, was destined for the scaffold, which he was to mount within the year, at the Bastille. For many years, Biron had been haunted by the advice of a fortune-teller, that he should 'beware the Burgundian blow'. In his final moments, he enquired as to the origins of his executioner. It came as no surprise to learn that the man was from Burgundy.

iv   Brothers in Arms

The Progress of 1601 was the most memorable of Elizabeth's reign. According to Stow, the Queen prided herself on having 'royally entertained' a royal ambassador 'in her subjects' houses'. It was an unforgettable time for Ralegh, who recalled it to his companions in 1618, on his way from Devonshire to the scaffold. How much of a part had Beaurepaire played in it? In 1686, a visiting herald compiled an inventory of its stained glass. There was a fine collection, particularly in the windows of 'the Chamber' and the 'Gallery Chamber'. (The arms were those of the King, of the great noble families and of the local gentry.) In addition, he refers to 'the windows of the Room called the Queens chamber alias corner Chamber'. The depictions here are of the Pexall, Brocas and Paulet arms, implying that the corner tower in question had been added, in the mid-1500s, by Sir Richard Pexall, whose wife was a Paulet. Had Queen Elizabeth been put up here in 1601 and lent the room her name?

Old Beaurepaire is illustrated on a plan of the estate that was drawn up for Edward Savage in 1613. There certainly seem to be two corner blocks, and a façade that is more Tudor than medieval. The size of the house can be judged from its Hearth Tax assessment, in 1665, when John Thorner, who married a Brocas widow, was in residence. With its thirty-nine hearths, Beaurepaire was comparable in size to The Vyne, which had been reduced by that date (following the demolition of the base court buildings) to forty-three. According to Savage's plan, there was a single bridge from the house across the south side of the moat, and, beyond it, a stable yard. These structures may still have been standing in the early 1800s, when Caroline Wiggett was a visitor. William Clift (born in 1828) says he could recall the building of the present bridge (which is on the east side), as the timber for it was cut down on his father's farm. According to Clift, the large iron gates at the end of the bridge were imported from Wokefield, so the works presumably date from about 1839, when that property was sold. As well as an earlier suspension bridge over the west side of the moat, there is now an additional foot-bridge over the north side, and a modern stable block has been erected on the farther bank.

With its thick walls and defensive moat, Beaurepaire was inevitably fortified during the Civil War, when the Brocases held it for the King. The then head of the family, Thomas Brocas, was a tragic figure, of apparently blameless character, who nevertheless languished for many years in the debtor's gaol. Through the entire duration of the hostilities, his wife Elizabeth was the spirited mistress of Beaurepaire. With a garrison consisting of 'two troops of horse and sixty musketeers', it became an outpost of Basing House, from which 'the country was plundered as far as Reading'. In November 1643, Sir William Waller's Parliamentary troops had descended on The Vyne, ready to impede a relief force under Sir Ralph Hopton. The stained glass from the Chapel, ripe for destruction by the fanatical Puritans, is supposed to have been stashed away in the Sher. The windows from Bramley Church are likewise said to have been preserved in the moat at Beaurepaire, and this was no doubt also true of the stained glass from the house.

Apart from its most prominent families - the Sandys, Brocases, Cufaudes and Beverleys - the locality was generally hostile to the King. That much is implied by the dashing Colonel Gage, who memorably brought relief to Basing in the autumn of 1644. In the account of his daring return journey to Oxford, he describes how,

'the more to amuse the enemy and give him cause to think that I thought of nothing less than so sudden a retreat, I sent out certain warrants that afternoon, which I knew would fall into the enemy's hands, to the towns of Sherborne and Sherfield, to bring speedily a certain quantity of corn into Basing House, upon pain (if they refused) of sending them 1000 horse and dragoons to set their towns on fire before next day at noon.'

Loyalties were divided within the house of Brocas itself. Whilst the heir, Robert, was with his King at Oxford (and mysteriously murdered there in 1643), the second son, Thomas, was a Captain in the Parliamentary army, a participant in the Siege of Banbury in 1644. A third son, William, was a Cavalier, killed at the first Battle of Newbury (20 August 1643). According to legend, William was in love with one of the Sandys girls, and was accused of neglecting his duty. Determined to live this down, he vowed in his next engagement to capture an enemy standard, or else to die in the attempt. His body was recovered from the field on the morning after the battle. Clutched in his hand was the yellow flag of Parliament (long afterwards displayed in the Banqueting House in Whitehall). The enemy standard bearer, from whom he had wrested it, lay dead at his side.

Heroic feats like those of Gage and Brocas were not enough to save the cause of the King in Hampshire. In April 1645, a detachment from the New Model Army drew up at the moat to take Beaurepaire's surrender. When further Parliamentary forces arrived, the gallant defenders 'quitted the house and fled to Basing, whither they were pursued with good execution done upon them, a welcome business to Barkshire and Hampshire'. Many of them must have perished at the bloody storming of Basing House that took place towards the end of the same year. To have had a son on the winning side doubtless proved a blessing for Thomas, and there is no evidence of any rift between them. The elder Thomas was in any case in a vulnerable position: in 1648, he was still 'a prisoner in the King's Benche for greate debts, and havinge little or nothing to subsist on but what was before limited to him for his life, which if the creditors did seize on, he would perish for want of a livelihood'. His miserable life ended in 1663. By their own account, the family had ruined themselves in the service of Charles I, but little gratitude was shown to them by his restored son. It seems that Thomas Brocas went so far as to claim a peerage by way of reward; he was offered only a baronetcy, and declined it 'in terms which were considered by the Crown lawyers as punishable'. At least he had held on to Beaurepaire, which he was to pass on to his grandson, the son of the Parliamentary captain, whose name was also Thomas.

v   Family Portraits

The Brocases may have lost all their plate in the war, but they had preserved their stained glass and had gained a picture of Charles I, a token gift from 'His Most Sacred Majesty'. According to Burrows, the family historian, the portrait was 'an excellent copy of some master, exactly like what Charles was in the habit of giving to his friends'. This and many other family heirlooms were removed from Beaurepaire after the death of Thomas. His granddaughter Jane, only surviving child of the murdered Robert, took them to the Gardiner family into which she had married (a female-line descendant of which, the Earl Jellicoe, is also the Viscount Brocas).

There was the portrait, for example, of a 'dark, stern man in armour', thought to be Robert himself. A more arresting image, though, was that of Robert's grandfather, Sir Pexall Brocas. Sir Pexall was never able to live at Beaurepaire, which his step-relatives, the Savages, had so cunningly settled upon themselves. He was brought up at Swakeleys in Ickenham, and, when of age, lived mostly in London (in St Bride's), keeping Steventon as his country seat. He was knighted by the new King, James I, on his first coming down to London. The 'divers knights' appointed on that occasion are said by Camden to have been 'promiscuously created', and Pexall himself was certainly a poor candidate for the honour. The King had soon afterwards to pardon him for riots (probably in support of the Essex rebellion in 1601) and for 'forging and publishing a forged deed of perjury'. Not surprisingly, Sir Pexall's petition to attend the Coronation as Master of the King's Buckhounds went unanswered (as, indeed, did that of Dymoke, the King's Champion). As Burrows puts it, 'we cannot but suspect that even James, with all his coarseness, found the character of the hereditary Master too bad to permit of public recognition, and was devising some other method of managing his buckhounds'.

Apart from engineering his own financial ruin, Sir Pexall's chief notoriety was as an adulterer. He is said to have fathered between seventy and a hundred bastards. His contemporary, the London historian John Stow, records that

'On Sunday, October 24, 1613, Sir Pecsall Brocas did open penance at Paul's Cross; he stoode in a white sheete, and held a stick in his hand, having been formerly convicted before the High Commissioners for secret and notorious adulteries with divers women.'

Far from being chastened by so humiliating a sentence, Sir Pexall seemed keen to attract attention. Later tradition has it that he was attended by 'thirty men in scarlet that waited upon him to the Lord Mayor, when he went to demand a dinner after doing penance'!

It is scarcely credible that such a man should have drawn up in 1610, with all legal formality, an ambitious scheme whereby he would 'found a Colledge at Oxford to be called Brocas Colledge'. Perhaps the whole thing was a joke, a means of getting himself him talked about. (However, a great-grandson, Bernard Gardiner, was to become Vice-Chancellor of the University in 1714, an irony that Sir Pexall would have relished.) Fortunately, the Brocas family was able in 1626 to return to Beaurepaire, in the person of the unlucky Thomas. He was Sir Pexall's only legitimate son, upon whom he had wisely been persuaded to settle the estate. Sir Pexall may therefore have been an occasional visitor. When he died in 1630, he was buried with his ancestors in St Andrew's Church. It is regrettable that the grave is unmarked: no more colourful figure has ever been associated with the parish.

The portrait of Sir Pexall, by an anonymous artist, showed him as the 'foppish debauchee' that he undoubtedly was, 'with long hair flowing over the monstrous collar of the period, elaborately worked with the Brocas lion alternating with the crest of the Moor's head and Oriental crown'. In his wife's portrait, by Cornelius Janssen, her 'pale and rather handsome face, and gentle eyes, tell their own story'. Another Gardiner heirloom was the portrait of a favourite retainer, inscribed by a later generation with the words, 'Hodge, Jester to Sir Pexil Brocas of Beaurepaire'. Hodge is said to have been the last professional jester in private service in England - further proof of Sir Pexall's vanity and love of a joke. His face, according to Burrows, is that of a 'rough, humorous fellow, something like an old-fashioned roadside innkeeper'.

Other notable paintings remained with the Brocases at Beaurepaire, where Caroline Wiggett may have seen them. There was, for example, a forbidding likeness of Sir John Savage, proudly attired as Master of the Queen's Buckhounds. Another portrait, ascribed to Vandyke, was said to be of 'Earl Strafford, beheaded May 12, 1641'. There were also portraits, believed to be originals, of 'Bloody' Mary and of Mary, Queen of Scots. More satisfying to young Caroline, however, was the Brocas monument in Bramley Church, in which the 'old-fashioned' lady of her acquaintance was cast in a new light, as the beautiful young wife who tenderly supports her expiring husband. The sculpted figures are both dressed in classical garb (Mrs Brocas wears a veil), although the portly Mr Brocas retains the fashionable periwig of his own era. The work is variously ascribed to Thomas Banks, R.A., or to Thomas Carter the younger, who was in the area at the time, still working in 1780 on the monument to Speaker Chute at The Vyne.

The Brocas tomb was originally placed in the open air in Bramley churchyard. Since 1802, it has been housed in a brick chapel attached to the south side of the church, on the site of a former Lady Chapel. It was designed for Mrs Brocas by the future Sir John Soane, one of the foremost architects of his day and a native of Whitchurch. In 1809 she had sadly to add a memorial to her adopted step-son, Bernard Austin Brocas, a Captain in the Berkshire Militia, whose five young children were the future hope of the Brocases. The matriarch of the family, who had suffered her fair share of personal tragedy and loneliness, appears always to have conducted herself in grand seignorial style, which even then made her a considerable curiosity. One wonders whether she persisted in wearing the hoop, an uncomfortable, outmoded accessory that was still being endured by older women. That alone would have endeared her to Mr Chute, and have made her seem 'old fashioned' to young Caroline.

CHAPTER FOUR

Church and Village

i   Mud and Thatch

Almost entirely owned and controlled by these two eccentrics, Sherborne in the early 1800s had been unaffected by modernity, to an extent that their contemporaries found shocking. The cottages of the peasantry were in many cases hundreds of years old, but were too dilapidated to be considered charming. All were constructed in the traditional fashion, around timber frames. The walls of some of them had been infilled with brick but mostly they consisted of mud and manure; the roofs were usually of thatch. There would have been plenty of gaps in both to admit the wind and the rain. Some of the cottages in Sherborne had only one bedroom and few would have had more than two. They were dismally inadequate housing for families that were frequently large.

The connecting roads were generally a sea of mud. Horses and cattle passed to and fro in areas where they are never seen today. For most of the time there would have been a busy air about the place, for Sherborne was a community at work. Almost everyone was employed either at or close to home. The workshops of the various tradesmen - the carpenter, miller, blacksmith, tailor, shoemaker, brewer and so on - were scenes of noise and activity. There were numerous children about the place, as there was no school to keep them occupied. With so little space in their cottages, the women did as much of their work as was possible (such as their washing) in the open air. At least they were spared having to lug bucket-loads of water from some distant pump. Sherborne was better placed than most villages in the abundance of its springs. Many of its old properties are still equipped with their original wells, piped water having been introduced to the village as recently as 1940. As for the village streams, they may have seemed 'pretty' to Caroline Wiggett, but how convenient they must have seemed in the absence of sewers!

Much of the village would have been considered unwholesome by anyone claiming gentility. It is only relatively recently that the characteristic workman's cottage has come to be appreciated for its architectural and historical interest, deemed worthy of preservation, and, indeed, regarded as a desirable place to live. Most of the old houses in Sherborne were blithely demolished in the nineteenth and twentieth centuries, by landowners who were unencumbered by sentiment. The best surviving examples are those clustered around the Swan Meadow, including 'The Swan' itself. Significantly, these survivors are for the most part properties, like 'The Swan', that were never owned by the Chutes.

April Cottage, backing onto Swan Meadow, is one of these low thatched buildings, typical of old Sherborne at its most picturesque. Historically, it was a dwelling for paupers. Considered hugely inconvenient, it only narrowly escaped demolition after its purchase by the Vyne estate in about 1897. A number of no less interesting buildings has nevertheless vanished within living memory. These include the partly-thatched Mill Cottages at Mill End, demolished in 1963, a pair of partly-thatched cottages at Lillydown, at the western extremity of the village, demolished in the 1970s to make way for a modern house and garage, and a cottage on the site of a bungalow next to the Old Post Office, which went in 1978 or 9. These were typical of the houses that, two hundred years ago, were to be seen throughout the parish, but which were probably half fallen down even then.

ii   Church Parade

The Chute family at The Vyne considered themselves to be physically remote from the village, so great store was set by their attendance at church on Sundays, particularly as an opportunity to renew their contacts with the poor. These were state occasions, the family setting out in style in a gorgeous carriage, decidedly a mark of affluence in those days. According to Caroline it had a barouche box at the rear and was drawn, like Mrs Brocas's, by a team of black horses. The party was accompanied by Charles, the coachman, smartly attired in 'a yellow jacket, leathers, and black jockey cap'. Characteristically, Mr Chute preferred to drive the vehicle himself, riding postillion.

The gravel drive which he had created in 1808 had extended from Vyne Lodge Farm to the bottom of Swingate Hill, where a 'swing gate' (which he replaced) marked the traditional entrance to the estate. The brook which passes beneath the road at this point had in those days to be forded, to the frequent discomfort of the horses. The remaining part of the journey into the village, which involved the negotiation of a steep hill, was unlikely to be smooth, quick or easy.

There can have been very little traffic passing in and out of the village (in contrast to today), and that at a snail's pace. Wiggett Chute recalled his uncle's carriage being stuck in the mud on one occasion, by what is now the entrance to Vyne Meadow (there would have been fields on either side). The physical transformation of Church End in the past two centuries has been total: such former landmarks as survive have been altered beyond recognition. As they descended into the village, Mr Chute's party would have passed, on their left hand side, an ancient two-storey cottage. Wiggett Chute was to replace it with the handsome single-storey building of today, designed as almshouses but now a private dwelling (Nos.18 and 20 Vyne Road). It was to the old cottage on the site that Bush, the faithful butler at The Vyne, was eventually to retire with his wife, Mrs Bush turning her hand to running a small school.

The next building on that side (No.16 Vyne Road), still with a thatched roof but with a modernised exterior, was erected by William John Chute in 1823. There is no upper floor, for it was purpose-built as a classroom. Here, Eliza Chute was able in reasonable comfort and with Caroline's assistance to conduct her cherished Sunday School. The Sherborne Sunday School, 'then an almost unheard of thing', had been opened in 1816, meeting at first in a pair of cottages. The boys were separated into one and the girls into the other. For lack of space, they had later decamped to what is now Edernish House, but were eventually driven out by the cold. A degree of comfort was important: the sessions went on for most of the day, there being only one service on a Sunday. Such schools, promoted since 1780 by the printer Robert Raikes, provided a general rather than an exclusively religious education (no other form of schooling was available to Sherborne children), and were the origin of the modern, universal system. Wiggett Chute was to build a schoolhouse elsewhere. The former Sunday School premises, which the ladies had made 'very pretty with its garden and porch', were converted first into additional almshouses and, later, into a private dwelling.

At the foot of the hill, the road was crossed by an open stream which Wiggett Chute was to cover over - a pity, as today it would have been regarded as picturesque, and might have had the effect of slowing the traffic. Walkers may have stepped over it by means of some curious Sarsen stones that had somehow been washed up here at the end of the Ice Age. (Three of them are propped up on the verge, outside Nos.6, 8 and 10 Vyne Road, whilst another is to be found on the island in the Square, opposite the Post Office.) The open stream, which would only have added to the slipperiness of the road, was understandably regarded as a major inconvenience.

There are said to have been further obstructions in the form of the 'many old cottages' which, in Caroline's words, 'intercepted the road', as well as 'a small kiln which was in the way, and certainly no ornament, that was removed in my Uncle's time'. The old cottages to which she refers may include Nos.6, 8 and 10 Vyne Road, which are visibly built round timber frames, though they now have the benefit of bricked-in walls and tiled roofs. The backs of these cottages appear in a view of the village (from Dancer's Meadow) which Caroline sketched in 1816. They have thatched roofs and, in one case, a dormer window.

Furthermore, there were two, now vanished buildings on the opposite side. Where the road bends at the bottom of the hill was 'a little tumbledown old single cottage', destined to be purchased and demolished by Wiggett Chute. Was this the cottage on the hill that was traditionally occupied by a shepherd, after which it was sometimes known as 'Shepherd's Hill'? Almost next to it on the roadside, straddling the stream where it flows into the garden of Edernish House, was a more substantial building, today reduced to a few half-buried bricks. From another of Caroline's sketches (dated 1813), it appears to have been some sort of service building, no doubt the malthouse that is mentioned in 1789. There is possibly a stable or coach-house attached, and accommodation upstairs, which might have been for the coachman or grooms.

The house which this building would have served, set back a little from the road, still survives, but has been considerably altered and extended. Edernish House is its modern name. It was the Rectory House from about 1840 until 1975, but when Caroline was a child was called 'Tally's'. Her sketch from 1816 shows it to have been a plain-fronted house of two storeys. A property of Mrs Brocas, it was uninhabited and 'in a dilapidated state, the windows all broken and looking forlorn'. This was a gentleman's residence, for which there seems to have been a lack of suitable tenants. It had only recently become deserted, though. The previous occupant, in whose time the house appears to have been rebuilt, was Francis John Martelli (probably a Florentine), the steward or land agent to John Chute: it was not only works of art that John had imported from Italy! A poignant inscription on the floor of the church remembers Isabella, the four-year-old daughter of Francis and his wife Ann (presumably an Englishwoman), who had died in 1762. In 1767, Martelli was said to be aged about fifty and to have been in John Chute's service for upwards of fourteen years. He was reported in that year for being one of only four Roman Catholics in the village, his co-religionists being the Widow Starle, 'a very ancient and poor woman, whose husband was a Papist', and her two spinster daughters, Mary and Jane. Martelli may have been regarded with some suspicion, and was certainly an inconsiderate neighbour. In 1789, Charles Tubb from next-door (Tubb's holding, Andrews' Farm, is presumed to have been on the church side of Martelli's property) complained that he was using his yard as a means of access. Martelli was found also to have 'frequently stop'd the stream of water running under his Malthouse to the detriment of the Road and the neighbourhood'. 'Tally' was the best effort of the locals at pronouncing his name; they obviously had as much difficulty with Italian as they had with French.

Martelli's house had arisen on the site of an earlier building known as Egerton's Farm. Up to the middle of the eighteenth century, it had been occupied by three generations of the Egerton family - Joseph, Ezekiel, and another Joseph. The first Joseph had, in the 1720s, been Thomas Brocas's diligent steward, jealously protecting his rights against the Chutes, who regarded him as an 'Impudent fellow'. He seems also to have managed the glebe on behalf of the vicar, Mr Lyon. The name is commemorated in Egerton's (or 'Little Morgaston') Wood, once part of the same holding, which was planted in the nineteenth century, after its acquisition by Wiggett Chute, as a means of screening The Vyne from the Aldermaston Road.

It was only on Sundays (at least until 1823, when William John Chute built the thatched schoolhouse at the top of the hill) that Tally's came to life. Mrs Chute and her niece would repair to it after the morning service with the Sunday School. There were two main rooms divided by a passage, into which the boys and girls could be conveniently segregated. In the winter-time, even with the fires lit, it could be 'very cold work', according to Caroline, but was 'otherwise comfortable, being near the church, and more to ourselves'.

iii   The Heart of Darkness

In what is now the garden of Springfield House, across the road from Tally's, was another old house that has since vanished. From Caroline's sketch, the house appears to have been at right angles with the road and was probably set back from it. In the 1840s it was occupied by a baker, who would insist on slaughtering his pigs in full view of the Rectory. Above it, on the corner, was a modest thatched cottage, running lengthwise along Dark Lane. Heavily disguised, the cottage may in part still exist as the original core of Springfield House, the Edwardian villa which has been built around it. The corner cottage also features in Caroline's sketch and in a view of the Square (from the entrance to Tally's), which was painted, possibly by Eliza Chute, in 1837. In both pictures, it is enclosed by a neat picket fence.

In the early nineteenth century, villagers would have perceived the so-called 'Dark Lane' as their route to Basingstoke. It is actually marked as such on old maps, and was the route taken by the coaches that came up Elm Road and turned in the Square for their journey back to the town. (The countryside as far as the Holy Ghost Chapel was of course completely undeveloped.) 'Dark Lane' seems a misnomer for such a pretty, sunny spot, and, unsurprisingly, is not its proper name. The true Dark Lane is the one that approaches Kiln Farm from the Sherborne Road, indeed a gloomy, sunken thoroughfare, surrounded by high hedgerows that blot out the sun. The lane leading off the Square is correctly called 'Church Lane', after the Church Cottages - the now prettified April Cottage - which were a pair of one-up-one-down dwellings, maintained by the parish overseers as accommodation for the destitute. The name was misappropriated by the council in 1960, supposedly to discourage traffic along the lane, presumably because of its sinister connotations!

Weight of traffic was not a concern in the early 1800s. For most people, those who went everywhere on foot, there seems to have been an alternative route to Basingstoke that avoided the original 'Dark Lane'. Today, a footpath leads through the yard and garden of the pub and across Ten-Acre Piece (the field behind Vidler's Farm), where it meets the Sherborne Road. The original short-cut is likely to have skirted, rather than crossed the open field, which, according to Clift, was usually the case with footpaths. If this was a long-established trackway, much used by villagers, it would explain why the pub faces east and Swan Cottage opposite faces west, whilst next-door Maple Tree Cottage faces south, directly onto its former course. The so-called 'Top Road', which cuts through Ten-Acre Piece to connect with Elm Road, is an early by-pass, the creation of Wiggett Chute, probably in the early 1830s. According to local tradition, Wiggett had it in for the pub, perhaps because he thought it unduly tempting to travellers at the end of their journey. His aversion to 'beershops' in general is a matter of record. Wiggett nevertheless used to chair the annual supper of the Sherborne Cricket Club at 'The Swan', so cannot have been opposed to it entirely.

iv   Metamorphosing Houses and Moths

The old road is regrettably not marked on any map, nor are there any pictures of it, but there is abundant information about the Square. It was crossed by a pair of tracks which formed three central triangles of grass, instead of the modest island of today. The road surfaces appear to have been deeply uneven and stoney. On the site of the Post Office was a thatched cottage, its timber frame infilled with brick, that bears a striking resemblance to Swan Cottage: the work, no doubt, of the same seventeenth-century builder. There was a single-storey thatched building to the right of it.

The house on the west side of the Square, now known as The Haye, dates from the same period: an internal beam is inscribed with the year '1671'. Never a possession of the Chutes or Brocases, it is supposed in its early days to have been a Quaker meeting-house and place of burial. The graves, many of them marked by stones, are said to have extended from the present kitchen of The Haye into what became the next-door garden (that of the schoolmaster), but which, until 1885, was within the bounds of the property. (The remains of a woman and two children were discovered there in the 1970s, to great consternation.) Around the year 1902, the house underwent a dramatic, Lutyens-esque transformation, and has been generally aggrandised. When Caroline sketched it, The Haye was a humble-looking building, visibly timber-framed and with a jettied upper floor. It was divided into two tenements, which were occupied in 1818 by James Gibbons and Edward Jennings. The freeholder was Daniel Hasker, the village maltster, who sold it in that year to Charles White, the village tailor, for a mere five shillings. By 1837, White had removed the quaint jetty and had faced the entire building in stucco. He had also erected a large sign, facing onto the Square, announcing his trade, in which he had presumably prospered.

The double cottages which have metamorphosed into The Haye had formerly been possessions of the Moth family, one of the oldest in Sherborne. Oliver Mothe witnessed a grant in the 1190s, and the names of his descendants abound in the early Brocas deeds. An Edward Mothe was Rector from 1541 to 1554. The seat of the family was the dwelling on the corner of the Aldermaston and Monk Sherborne Roads, traditionally known as 'Moth's House', but renamed 'Weybrook House' in the later 1800s, when it was made somewhat smarter. The present building dates from the seventeenth century, but the Moths had lived on the site since at least 1409.

William Moth, describing himself as a Gentleman, died in 1738, leaving an annuity to 'the poor people of my parish', but specifically excluding the Benhams, who lived on the site of Weybrook Cottage. The tone of his will is generally sour, as he complains elsewhere of his great losses and debts. Whether for financial reasons or as a matter of principle, his executors were unwilling to pay burial fees to the minister. After ten days of argument, the body was interred 'in a close of ground without any funeral ceremony'. William's final resting-place was high on Rooksdown, beside the Kingsclere Road, a suitably bleak position for an outcast. Moth's Grave appears on a late-eighteenth-century map and was formerly marked by the Five Firs that blew down in about 1940.

William's heir, his cousin of the same name, died in 1769. He, too, was childless, and left the various Moth properties (not only in Sherborne St John but in Monk Sherborne, Tadley, Baughurst and Stratfield Mortimer) to his widow, Mary. Mrs Moth promptly acquired a second husband, Thomas Stubbs, Esq., sometime of Westminster, Basingstoke and Poole, and bore him a brace of sons. Whilst Moth's House was let out to the well-known Lyford family (of doctors), both Stubbs boys joined the infantry and served in the Peninsular War. The elder son, Thomas William, was one of the British officers - a Major-General no less - who ran the Portuguese army, and of whom Wellington had a generally low opinion; George, the younger, a Captain in the 61st Foot, was killed in 1812, at the Battle of Salamanca. General Stubbs severed all his connections with Sherborne when he sold off the estate, by public auction at the Crown Inn, Basingstoke, in 1817. Moth's House and other lands were bought by Nathaniel Loader, a draper in the town, whilst The Haye went to the Hasker family, who had been leaseholders of the property since 1774.

The Moth holdings had extended out of the Square along Elm Road, which even now is sometimes referred to as 'Moss Hill', a corruption of 'Moth's Hill'. Until the closure of Rooksdown Lane in 1972, locals thought of it as the road to Wootton. In the early 1800s, a property on the corner of Crane's Road, consisting of a farmhouse and buildings set in an acre of land, was still occupied by a branch of the family, less exalted than the senior Moths but their acknowledged kinfolk. The present house on the site, which has a much reduced garden, is called Abbotsfield. Owing to the still active springs in the area, the adjacent highway had effectively to be forded in winter-time. All around it were the open fields, those to the west being known as 'The Severalls'. The Abbotsfield site had been bequeathed to Richard Moth senior (died 1763), an illiterate labourer, in the will of his cousin, old William, along with a moiety of Oakridge Farm. However, the family could hardly be said to have flourished: when they eventually moved out in 1827, the buildings at Moth's Farm were described as 'all falling down'. Although there are none living in the village today, the telephone directory lists Moths at Winchfield and Kingsclere and at other places in the area, the perhaps unwitting heirs to an ancient line.

v   Manor and Glebe

The Square, into which Elm Road led, was the focal point of the village, especially as the location of the parish church. Between The Haye and the churchyard was the then much wider opening to the Church Path. The direct route to West End, it was known in the eighteenth century as Vicarage Lane, and was probably frequented, throughout its length, by vehicles, horses and cattle, as well as pedestrians. (Repairs had been ordered in 1789, when the walls of the adjacent fish ponds were said to be in a 'very ruinous state and dangerous to passengers'.) The Haye at that time faced onto the churchyard (an original front door survives but is never used) across a much narrower front garden. It was extended into the lane in 1885, in exchange for an equivalent strip of land at the side, part of the old Quaker burial-ground.

Near the opening to the lane, 'an old May pole stood on a sort of green and some old stocks'. The Maying was an ancient fertility festival, apparently extinct in Sherborne as in most parts of England, though still occasionally observed in Bramley, where 'young girls in straw bonnets and white gowns, and their lovers in their Sunday attire,' would dance through 'covered alleys built of green boughs, decorated with garlands and great bunches of flowers'. Mary Russell Mitford, who describes the scene in *Our Village*, felt herself transported to some 'modern Arcadia'. Typically, the Sherborne Maypole was considerably higher than the nearby church. The adjacent stocks, and whipping post, were a less pleasant relic of the past. Until not so long ago, they had been used to punish petty offenders such as drunkards and blasphemers, or breakers of the Sabbath (including those tempted to work on their allotments). In Sherborne, as elsewhere, these, too, had fallen into disuse.

Along the eastern side of the churchyard, a lane led, as now, to the Manor farmhouse. On the edge of the lane, where there is now a dense clump of yews and firs, there was then a tumbledown cottage, a church house, which is mentioned in a document of 1634. It was occupied by the parish clerk, Smallbones, and his large family. Directly opposite were an old barn and some agricultural buildings, probably part of the smallholding called Andrews' Farm (known to have been next door to Edernish House), that was occupied from 1782 by the Tubb family. Timbers from these vanished buildings appear to have been recycled in the smart pair of cottages that has replaced them (Rosemary and Elderberry Cottages). Their gardens back onto the modern Rectory, on the site of what for centuries was the parish or 'hundred' pound. Stray cattle would be rounded up by the hayward and held here until their owners collected them, on payment of an appropriate fine.

Manor farmhouse, on the north side of the church, looked very different then, for it was rebuilt in 1828. The earlier building still survives as the back part of the house. Low and compact, it is probably 'the farmhouse' with three hearths that was recorded in 1665. The farmyard was at the front: there were stables on one side and sheds on the other. After a fire in 1875, the farm buildings were reconstructed in their present position, and replaced by a neat gravel approach, more in keeping with the raised status of the house. Manor Farm was occupied then and for more than a hundred years afterwards by a branch of the Bramley Clifts, who seem to have been highly regarded at The Vyne.

The farm pond to the west of the house is almost certainly medieval. Manor Farm may well have originated as the 'demesne', or home farm, of the Ports and St Johns: so large a fishpond suggests that its early occupants were themselves of high standing. On Anthony Chute's estate map (*c.* 1732) it is described as the 'Manor House of Sherborne St John', in remembrance, perhaps, of former glory. There was certainly a belief locally that it had been the site of a great house, based on the presence of a substantial, stagnant moat on the north side, connecting to a corner of the pond. (The greater part of it was drained and filled in

1862, the remaining part only a few years ago.) The 'moat' may always have had some agricultural rather than defensive purpose: on the other hand, small, moated manor-houses are by no means unusual in the area, Beaurepaire, Cufaude and Sherfield being the nearest examples.

The original Rectory House, which was on the opposite (south) side of the churchyard, had also been reduced to a farmhouse. Described as 'very old and dilapidated', it was occupied by the tenant of the glebe lands. 'It and the very various farm buildings belonging to it stood on the site of the present school and yard and road,' writes Wiggett Chute. Caroline knew it as 'Merton's Farm', after the tenant, who was later succeeded by John Helston. The house had long been considered unsuitable accommodation for a Rector, and the preferment had become, in his absence, a sinecure, without day-to-day responsibility for the cure of souls. The Rector in Caroline's childhood was none other than her 'uncle', Thomas Vere Chute, who lived in Norfolk. The administration of the parish was traditionally entrusted to a vicar or other appointee. The current incumbent, the Rev. James Austen, was himself the Rector of Steventon.

The same 'parsonage house' had consisted in 1634 of 'a hall, a parlour, a kitchin, a milkhouse, a buttery, foure upper roomes, a studdy, a Cutting' [*i.e.* catslide roof] at ye end of ye kitchin, a garden, an Orchard, a backside [and] a fish pound'. It was listed as having six hearths in 1665. There were also a 'great barne of foure baies, with a Carthouse at ye end of it, a Cowstall, a Stable, a little barne, a house or yard and a gatehouse'. It was into this yard that Mr Chute would drive up of a Sunday and park his coach, and here that the vicar, too, would put up his horse, having ridden over from Steventon to take the service. Caroline speaks of going into the churchyard 'between two barns or stables' (the lych gate dates only from 1888). The whole complex was demolished in about 1840, admittedly in a good cause. Wiggett Chute founded the still-flourishing Sherborne school on the site. With characteristic thrift, he constructed much of the new building using typical two-inch Tudor bricks, remnants, probably, of the former Rectory's great chimney-stacks. Remains said to be of his coach-house can still be seen in the schoolyard, as Wiggett was reluctant to give up so convenient a parking space.

Although Mr Austen had no use for it, Sherborne's officiating minister had traditionally been accommodated in the Vicarage house, which was at the far end of the lane, at its junction with Crane's Road. Long known, unhistorically, as The Old Rectory, it is one of the oldest and best documented houses in the parish. Built in around 1575, it was a classic timber-framed building of three bays, with a central hall and hearth-passage. In 1634, it comprised 'a hall, a kitchin, a buttery, a milkhouse, three little upper roomes, a studdy, a Cuttinge at ye south end of ye house, an Orchard, a garden, a little barne built upon posts, a stable [and] halfe an Acre of Medow more or less adjoyninge to it'. The end bay containing the service wing was replaced in about 1700 (presumably following the appointment, in 1699, of the Rev. Ezekiel Lyon) by a graceful brick cross-wing, which is characteristic of the best age of English architecture. The main room downstairs (now the parlour) must have continued to serve as a kitchen, for its great crescent-shaped hearth includes the remains of a bread oven. The large room above, still with its elegant panelling, was the vicar's chamber.

The remaining Tudor structure, deemed thoroughly unsophisticated, was, at the same time, encased in brick. The bay at the opposite end of the house, the one containing the vicar's study, is missing, possibly demolished as part of the same works, though it is more likely to have survived until the late nineteenth century. According to tradition, rooms at the Old Rectory were wainscoted. One of the Chutes is supposed to have stripped the house of its fine linenfold panelling, and to have installed it instead at The Vyne. No one would still remember such a detail if it had occurred before the nineteenth century. The most likely culprit is Wiggett Chute, who, in the 1840s, fitted out a former bedchamber as his Library, introducing, with other borrowed items, linenfold panelling from an unspecified source.

Mr Lyon, the vicar who is probably responsible for renovating the house, died in 1732, and is buried in the church. A generous Latin inscription on the slab records his exile from France for reasons of religion. Lyon's successor, Alexander Lytton, endeavoured to cure the bodies of his parishioners as well as their souls, for he is said to have 'practised physic'. The next vicar, from 1747, was the Rev. Benjamin Huffum Pepper, apparently the last clergyman to have resided in the house. Pepper was living in 1765 at Downham in Wiltshire, but was said (by the curate who ran the parish) to be 'about to move from thence with his family to the vicarage at Sherborn St John'. He was buried at Dummer in 1791, so the house may already have been abandoned by the time of his death. Mr Austen was appointed soon afterwards.

In 1827, when Wiggett Chute inherited, the Vicarage house was occupied by a labourer. James and Charles Wyeth (perhaps the same labourer's sons) were in residence by 1842, the building having been divided into two tenements. Although evidence of that division remains, The Old Rectory has since reverted to a single dwelling; its 'half an acre of Medow' has been reduced, though, the Glebe House having been built upon it in 1999. Until the late 1940s, there were only two other houses on Crane's Road, and open country all the way to Basingstoke. There was Crane's Farm at one end, on the corner with the Aldermaston Road; and there was Spring Cottage at the other, formerly the parish workhouse. People referred to the road, no doubt with a shudder, as 'Workhouse Lane'.

vi   Pews and Precedence

The churchyard, almost an extension of the neighbouring farm, was treated with scant respect: it contained several yew trees and some fine elms, but was regularly used (until 1865) as a pasture for sheep. The Church itself was as shabby and forsaken as the houses of its clergy. Mrs Chute was to pay for various repairs, adding the present tall spire in 1834. The previous one was short and stubby. The last significant alteration to the building had been the addition, in 1533, of the porch. The medieval nave, chancel and tower were otherwise intact. As for the interior, it had been untouched for a century or more. St Andrew's bore no resemblance to the spacious and well-ordered church of today, a legacy of the Victorians.

Before 1854, when Wiggett Chute constructed the North Aisle, the seating and other furniture had been crammed into the original nave and chancel, which had been divided by a single, narrow aisle. To increase the claustrophobia, the old roof timbers were concealed by a crumbling lath and plaster ceiling, which sounds as though it was positively dangerous. The building was stuffy in the summer, and freezing cold in the winter.

Prominent among the interior features were the boxed pews of the ratepayers, which occupied the top end of the nave, on either side of the aisle. These were high, narrow and uncomfortable. In some cases, there was barely space to kneel. Whilst the ratepayers sat bolt upright in their allotted pews, the poor of the parish were segregated to the rear according to their sex. They perched on make-shift seats that were 'not much better than benches with backs', females on one side of the aisle, males on the other. Men were additionally accommodated in a gallery at the back. They included the best singers, loosely affiliated into a 'choir', accompanied by a band consisting of both wind and stringed instruments. The same band would have turned out for village occasions such as weddings. Caroline describes their music as 'primitive', though Wiggett was to recall some 'fine anthems' being sung there. A leading member of the choir was old James Wyeth, the carpenter at The Vyne. He lived in the former Vicarage House, and is the man who probably took out its Tudor panelling for Mr Chute. Wyeth is described as 'the prima donna', equal to singing treble on occasion, as well as being an accomplished flautist.

The seating arrangements in St Andrew's were much the same as in any country church. A bizarre and possibly unique feature, however, was the 'Esquire's Pew'. It was so far forward in the nave that it was almost in the chancel, both ends of the church being then on a single level. 'Our pew,' writes Wiggett Chute, 'was a large square room with a ceiling over it, and the only opening for the admission of air or light was given by some twisted rails just below the ceiling.' Caroline describes it as 'quite boxed in with rather a pretty twisted rail all around it, and the sides so high you could see nothing unless you stood up'. Even more remarkably, this was a double-decker pew, as there was an upper gallery, reached by a flight of steps. Whilst the Chutes languished below, the overhead pew belonged to the Brocases, although they no longer used it, having abandoned St Andrew's for Bramley. It was felt to be the best place to put a barrel organ which Caroline herself was to donate, and was also used by the children's choir, which, once a week, she would coach over the piano at The Vyne. Organ and choir must both have added to the comedy of the occasion, by creating a thunderous din for the boxed-in family below.

The origins of this extraordinary arrangement were long forgotten, though not an awareness of former quarrels. In the past, Chute and Brocas had probably had adjacent pews, but one or other of them must forever have been nudging his pew a little further forward, in an attempt to outrank his rival. Eventually, having crossed the line into the chancel, they must have agreed on a compromise in the form of the double-decker pew, 'in which arrangement,' says Wiggett Chute, 'the Brocas appear to have certainly got the upper hand'. One wonders what the parishioners had made of it. Needless to say, those sitting immediately behind the pew would have had no view at all.

The Brocases had received no more than their due, as they were an older and more distinguished family than the Chutes. They could even claim descent, through the Pexalls and Paulets, from the original lords of Saint John. At one time, in the fifteenth century, they themselves had been possessors of The Vyne, then regarded as the inferior of Beaurepaire.

They had suffered heavily for their Royalism, whilst the Chutes, loyal to Parliament, had prospered. Their manor-house had probably never recovered from its occupation in the Civil War. Thomas Brocas (father of the late Bernard, who rebuilt the house) was said by 1725 to be an infrequent visitor. He may well have felt that his rank and position in Sherborne had been usurped by his wealthier neighbour.

Disputes between them were inevitable, given the lack of any clean division between their respective lands, the arbitrary removal of stakes, and the infrequency of manorial courts (the parish was poorly administered even then!). Anthony Chute, who inherited in 1722, seemed concerned to root out some of the abuses. For example, as lord of the manor of Sherborne, he regarded the entitlement to impound stray cattle (a common nuisance in the days of open fields) as one of his more important prerogatives. In return, he took upon himself, as lord of the manor, the burden of maintaining highways and bridges. Brocas, whose lordships of Crane's and Beaurepaire had historically been subject to their own manor courts, was less inclined to acknowledge his paramountcy.

When Anthony discovered that the hayward, whose wages he paid, was failing to impound and report strays (they were being seized as windfalls by the tenants), he took decisive action. At a specially convened manor court, Farmer William Rice (whose house on the site of Weybrook Farm was occupied in 1732 by one Elliott, Rice having moved to Pamber) was presented for purloining and eating a stray sheep, in defiance of manorial custom. Unfortunately, the sheep in question had been found in Westend Field, in which the rights of Chute and Brocas were hopelessly intermixed. Paying one of his rare visits to Beaurepaire, Brocas learnt of the affair from his servant, Joseph Egerton, and was furious. On 20 February 1727, he dispatched a strongly-worded rebuke to his neighbour, reproving him for his lack of courtesy. 'My very great and early Regard for yr worthy family would not easily permit me to imagine it possible for one so descended to Act in such a manner,' he wrote sarcastically.

'Well might the Ghosts of my Ancestors rise to upbraid my Tameness, if I should quietly give up this Right of Ages, and submit to see the Mannors of Beaurepaire and Cranes stript of their privileges, far be it for me to encroach upon the smallest branch of yr prerogative. I covet not a single Inch of yr numerous Acres, but in return desire an undisturb'd enjoyment of my scanty few.'

Anthony Chute, much the cleverer man, replied at length.

'Peace be the names of your Ancestors, and mine, by whom (as I would unwillingly disturb them) I am in no apprehension of being disturbed, tho' might Indignation raise the dead. The Injustice you (thro' a mistake or wrong Information) charge me with I verily believe would incense my departed Predecessors as deeply as the Tameness you seem so much concern'd to avoid the Imputation of, could possibly do yours.'

The language of both correspondents, with their invocation of the ancestors, is suggestive of a long-standing antipathy between the two houses. Chute is confident, though, of having right on his side. He concludes with an equal measure of sarcasm:

'I will not despair of having you for my neighbour, your handsome fortune which you are pleas'd to call your scanty Acres seeming to have amply provided for your residence in this part of the world, tho' your Destiny at present forbids you ...'

Yet letters in the same vein continued to pass between them, all of them carefully preserved in the Chute archive. The most significant outcome of the quarrel seems to have been Brocas's desertion of St Andrew's (where his own parents were buried) in favour of St James's, Bramley. As for the pew, it was dismantled by Wiggett Chute in 1854. However, parts of it were removed to The Vyne and can be seen there - the twisted rails on the window-sills in the Chapel, the cornices on the bookshelves of the Library.

vii   Five Hundred and Fifteen Souls

'Uncle Chute always sat in the corner of the pew, I, on the opposite one, and Aunt Chute next to me,' writes Caroline. During the holidays, she might be joined there by her elder brother, Wiggett, and by the vicar's son, Edward, one of Caroline's few friends of her own age (the boys were a couple of years apart at Winchester and then at Oxford). Edward Austen-Leigh (as he became) paints a vivid picture of the Squire,

'standing upright, tilting his heavy folio Prayer-book on the edge of his high pew, so that he had to look up rather than down on it. There he stands, like Sir Roger de Coverley, giving out the responses in an audible voice, with an occasional glance to see what tenants were at church and what schoolboys are misbehaving; and, I am sorry to add, sometimes, when the rustic psalmody began its discord in the gallery, with a humour, which even church could not restrain, making some significant gesture to provide a smile from me and other young persons in the pew.'

Reassuringly for Mr Chute, attendance was generally good, probably a majority of the village population (515 in 1815), but there were many, especially among the men, who came unwillingly to church. In those days, the annual hiring agreement of farm labourers typically included an obligation to attend, not only on Sundays but on Ash Wednesday, Good Friday and Christmas Day (although there were only four opportunities in the year to take communion). They were not obliged to stay awake. All along the walls on the men's side, there were permanent stains that had been made by their heads as they slumbered.

The labourers and even some of the lesser farmers would appear in their best white smocks, an almost forgotten feature of old England. These were often elaborately embroidered and are said to have been as warm as they were picturesque. Smock-making was one of Sherborne's cottage industries: the last of the village women to be so employed died in

1914. The day-to-day smocks were of different colours according to one's parish. In Bramley they were green, but the colour of the Sherborne smock is sadly unrecorded. Best white smocks were to be brought out for the last time in 1878, by the sixteen men who carried Chaloner Chute from The Vyne to his grave.

The women had their own uniform, consisting of strong, flat shoes (in winter-time they might clatter into church on their pattens), a tight-sleeved, cotton gown, a necker-chief, and a winged cotton bonnet, drawn tightly round the head. Warm clothing was essential, especially in an age of harsher winters. The church was not then equipped with double doors, and a single stove provided the only heating. There were no lights, either, except for the pulpit candles, although there were additional windows that have since been blocked up. The clerk would only light the candles just before the sermon. The stove almost invariably smoked, adding to the general discomfort. It is not surprising that there was no evening service.

Although her view of the proceedings was severely limited, Caroline was never to for-get the experience of those Sundays. The oak pulpit, which is elaborately carved, stood about eighteen inches higher than at present. A magnificent piece of craftsmanship, made by Henry Sly in 1634, it was wholly unrecognised and unappreciated, having been paint-ed over many times and 'agreeably covered with red cloth'.

The chancel ahead of her was level with the nave until almost the end, where the altar was raised on a platform about four feet high. It was covered by 'a rather handsome red cloth fringed with yellow': could this have been the altar cloth that was donated by the Brocases in the late 1400s, which is known to have been still in use in 1686? The Communion rails, about six inches higher, were painted white. There were steps in the middle leading up to the altar, and on either side were the 'two large old chests' that con-tained the parish registers. (The registers are now safely stored at Winchester.) Nearby was 'a large stand with two *old* Bibles chained to it', by which she presumably means the three volumes of Foxe's *Martyrs,* then 'seriously dilapidated'. They had been the gift of William Jackman, vicar from 1652, who was most assuredly a Puritan.

With its lurid illustrations and subject matter, Foxe's anti-Catholic diatribe was hardly suitable for a young girl, but it might have interested her to read, under the year 1558, of Sir Richard Pexall, of Beaurepaire. Pexall was a Catholic and a loyal servant of 'Bloody' Mary. As Sheriff of Hampshire, it had been his duty to execute the heretic Bembridge at the stake. Much to his credit and to the annoyance of the Queen, he had withdrawn him from the flames in the nick of time, presumably as an act of mercy. Sherborne had been stoutly Puritan by the time of the Civil War and by 1725 there was said to be 'no popish family' in the parish, but the Reformation had had powerful opponents locally. The first Lord Sandys, who, as Lord Chamberlain, was Henry VIII's leading courtier, had retired to the The Vyne in disgust, there to embark on treasonable correspondence with a foreign power. During the 'Reign of Terror' that followed, he seems to have arranged the marriage of his near neigh-bour, William Cufaude of Cufaude, with Cardinal Pole's niece Marie, thereby removing her from danger. Pockets of Catholism survived into Elizabethan times and beyond. At Hillend Farm, whose occupants by 1613 were a family called Dickenson, there are recesses which are thought to have been for the concealment of priests. The descendants of William and Marie Cufaude were resolute Catholics until their extinction in the early 1700s, even count-ing among them an Augustinian nun, whose portrait is at The Vyne.

The men of the parish, at least, were now all but indifferent to religion. Later in the century, when attendance ceased to be compulsory, they stayed away in droves, leaving a congregation that consisted largely of women. Quite apart from the sheer physical discomfort, the services were hardly inspiring. Few, if any, took part in the responses. Many were unable to read. Smallbones, the clerk, seated below the clergyman's desk, would do his best, but was himself barely literate. His role in the proceedings was quite a dramatic one. As he was also the bassoonist in the band, he would have to walk up to the gallery after the last 'Amen', when no doubt all eyes were fixed on him. Caroline found him terrifying. During Lent, the children of the parish faced the ordeal of reciting the Catechism in front of him, before the first hymn. 'Children, come and say your Catechism,' he would say in a sonorous voice, and they would spill out of the pews, or come forward from the middle of the aisle (as there were insufficient seats for all the offspring of the poor). The dozen fortunate children who attended the Sunday School had seats around the altar, and wore a uniform provided by Mrs Chute, presumably consisting of white aprons or pinafores. Each would tremble with fear as he stepped forward to say his piece in turn, including Caroline and Edward. Otherwise the children must have been bored stiff. There was a lot of bad behaviour, and Smallbones was constantly administering harsh discipline with a stick. The worst troublemakers could expect to be beaten with the bell ropes after the service.

Caroline would amuse herself by looking at the servants in the pews immediately behind her. Well forward of 'the poor', they clearly ranked high in the village pecking order. There were Charles the coachman and Bush the butler, dapper George Hickson, the huntsman, and Cox, the kindly but incompetent bailiff, who used to welcome little Caroline at Vyne Lodge Farm, picking her up on occasion to show her the piglets. The first Mrs Cox, 'an old-fashioned, cross woman', died when Caroline was a child, but was replaced some years later by a former housekeeper, Mrs Blyth, 'a good sensible woman, but immensely *fat*'. The Coxes occupied one half of the dilapidated Tudor farmhouse (which had an adjacent brewhouse), whilst George and his wife lived in the other. (When the old farmhouse was demolished in 1832, to make way for three cottages, the builders discovered in the roof the skeleton of a cat still holding in its mouth the skeleton of a rat.)

Ahead of her, in the pews on the north side of the chancel, Caroline could observe 'old Mrs Tubb' and her daughters, one of whom was married to Clift of Manor Farm. There were Farmer Winton, too, and some of the Cannons family who lived at Crane's Farm. Opposite them sat 'old Mrs White', the tailor's wife, and her sister, 'old Hannah'. White himself was presumably a ratepayer, entitled to sit in one of the boxed aisle pews. Another would have been occupied by Farmer Tubb, one of the leading landholders on the manor.

Charles Tubb (born about 1764) was considered rather simple and was known from his favourite expression as 'Dimme soul'. Word had got round that Farmer Clift of Bramley was, on a certain day, to move his well at Holly Cross from one side of the house to the other. In other words, he was going to block up the old one and dig a replacement. Aware that, on rare occasions, granaries and barns were actually dragged to different positions on rollers (this was to happen at Weybrook Farm in 1830), Tubb wondered by what ingenuity the old well was to be taken out whole and brought to the other side. He therefore made a special journey to witness the spectacle. There was much laughter at his expense, and a brick in the well wall was inscribed 'C.T., 1798', in his honour. On another occasion,

Tubb discovered one of his farm boys lying down in a field when he should have been at harrow. 'Dimme soul, boy,' he said, 'if you don't get up I'll knock'ee down.'

One so hopes that, somewhere at the back, was that other figure of fun, Dr Lyford's wig-wearing *protégé*. Given his connection with Moth's House, it seems likely that the recipient of his generosity would have been a Sherborne man, the source of a little mirth on an otherwise joyless occasion.

viii   Language Barriers

There is no knowing whether Mr Austen preached a lively sermon. He would be dressed in a black gown and perhaps with powdered hair, though without the wig that he had worn in his youth. Before mounting the pulpit, he would change at his desk and hang the surplice for the gown over his pew. A graduate of St John's College, Oxford, James Austen (1765 - 1819) was an accomplished writer of both poetry and prose, who, as a young fellow of his college, had published his own weekly magazine. Unfortunately, none of his works could compare with those of Jane, his younger sister. Perhaps, like his father (whom he had succeeded in 1805 as Rector of Steventon), he kept a collection of his own sermons and used them again and again. In his speech there was probably a sprinkling of the archaisms used by other members of the family, that were written as they were pronounced. An example is their use of the word 'sennet' for sennight, a week. The Austens spoke with a refined, educated London accent, similar, we gather, to that of Pepys. This is apparent from James's poetry, where, for instance, he rhymes the words 'join' with 'thine'. So boil becomes 'bile', point 'pint' etc. 'Consider the lilies of the field: they *tile* not ...'

The Chutes were no doubt appreciative of his sermons, but the congregation in general may not have gained much from them. (The address which his son Edward gave at Mrs Chute's funeral in 1843, which was published, would certainly have gone over their heads.) An enthusiastic rider to hounds, James Austen was an old and intimate friend of the family. On Sunday afternoons, he could usually be expected for dinner at The Vyne, accompanied in time by young Edward, who himself went a-hunting from an early age. There would have been ample time beforehand (dinner was served at about 3.30 p.m.) for parochial duties. James may also have taken the opportunity to visit his disabled brother, George, and uncle, Thomas Leigh, who lived together in Monk Sherborne, in the pretty but cramped cottage of the Culham family. George was an epileptic and perhaps also deaf and dumb, whilst Thomas was described as an 'imbecile'. The Vicar of Monk Sherborne, Dr Hall, was well acquainted with the Austens, and would no doubt also have kept an eye on them. (When, in 1798, Mrs Hall had given birth to a stillborn child, the result of a 'fright', Jane Austen wrote to her sister that she must have 'happened unawares to look at her husband', a remark which seems shocking by modern standards. It has been argued, though, that this was less an instance of Jane's malice than of deliberate bad taste, intended for humorous effect.) The haven of the two invalids, which has since been extended and is called Apple Tree Cottage, lies just out of the village of Sherborne St John, on the left-hand side of the Monk Sherborne Road.

All the Austens were known at The Vyne, as is apparent from their own correspondence and from the diaries of Eliza Chute. For instance, she records her first meeting with the family in 1793. The vicar had come to call, bringing with him old Mr and Mrs Austen and one of their daughters. The 'Miss Austin' to whom she refers may have been Cassandra, but Jane is sure to have visited at other times. They would in any case often meet at balls or at informal dinner parties, the Chutes being occasional guests at Steventon Rectory. Oddly, Jane never warmed to them. She reveals in her private letters, which are full of barbed comments about acquaintances, a low opinion of them both. 'William Chute called here yesterday,' she writes in 1796. 'I wonder what he means by being so civil.' In 1800 she reports a meeting with Eliza and her sister at Deane: 'They had meant to come on to Steventon afterwards but we knew a trick worth two of that.' Did she find them condescending? Was she jealous or resentful? It may have been too painfully obvious that, in contrast to her own position, they had money but no sense. She evidently preferred Tom Chute, James's close friend and contemporary, reporting to her sister that she had danced with him five times at a local ball. She knew Caroline, too, and was well aware of her situation. 'I am sorry to hear of Caroline Wiggett's being so ill,' she writes in 1817. 'Mrs Chute I suppose would almost feel like a mother in losing her.'

The despised Chute household may nevertheless have inspired certain characters and incidents in her novels. For instance, could it be Mr Chute's arrival in the county, 'a single man in possession of a good fortune', that is immortalised in the famous opening passage to *Pride and Prejudice*? Does not Mrs Chute's enthusiastic description of a trip to Box Hill, recounted to James and by him to Jane, seem to resurface as an episode in *Emma*? Above all, are not the circumstances of Fanny Price in *Mansfield Park* identical to those of young Caroline? The Chutes made an impact locally that not even Jane could ignore.

Families like the Brocases, Chutes and Austens, with their fine clothes, their education and connections, were separated from the ordinary country folk by a gaping chasm. There was, though, a general acceptance of one's lot in life, on the grounds that it had been ordained by God. James Austen's view of the lower orders, expressed in one of his poems, is that they were 'the nine parts of mankind' who were 'designed' for labour. With his quaint, courtly accent, he quite literally spoke a different language to his flock. The villagers communicated in the historic, now almost lost dialect of the West Saxons - once the language of kings - which had its own distinctive vocabulary and grammatical forms. 'In my youth,' writes Austen-Leigh, 'the old Hampshire peasants still used the word "abin" for "because".' In isolated places such as Selborne, and perhaps Sherborne too, pure Anglo-Saxon usages still prevailed, such as the plural ending '-en'. Thus people would speak of 'housen' instead of 'houses'. More commonly, though, they would add '-és' to a word. The plurals of 'beast', 'ghost' and 'post' would therefore be 'beastés', 'ghostés' and 'postés'. For 'its' they would say 'his' or 'hisen', for, in Hampshire, proverbially, 'everything is called he, except a Tom-cat'. (That peculiarity at least is still current in the Isle of Wight, as the author, having grown up there, can attest.) 'Be'est a gwine to vyer?' they might say. 'Are you going to the fair?' Today it seems like a foreign language. Fortunately it was one in which Mr Austen himself was fluent, having been brought up among the servants and villagers of Steventon. Its killing off in the course of the nineteenth century is a process in which Sherborne St John School no doubt played its part.

It was strongly felt by families like the Austens and Chutes that their comfortable positions in life brought with them a reciprocal obligation towards the poor. 'In those days there was such poverty,' writes Caroline, 'such as is not known in these days, I am happy to say.' Always first to leave the church, the Chutes would make a point of speaking to the poor folk about their health and the general welfare of the village. Charity was dispensed from The Vyne on a regular basis, as it would have been for many centuries past. In the winter months, at eight o'clock every morning, Mrs Chute would preside in person over a soup kitchen, filling each jug with broth from a large copper in the larder. There were annual distributions of Bath cloaking for the women and of swan down waistcoats for the men. The Chutes were generous hosts on many special occasions, such as the half-yearly audits, at which the tenants, announced as 'Farmer So and So', would file in turn into the Print Room, and proceed to mutter their excuses as to why they were unable to pay. In return they would be given both dinner and supper in the Steward's Room, where, according to Caroline, an amused observer, they 'kept up their merriment to a late hour'. Other treats for the villagers were national festivals. On a lovely October day in 1810, in honour of King George's Jubilee, the 'poor' were feasted on tables that were spread up the Avenue in front of the house, two old villagers being placed top and bottom with crowns on their heads. On 7 July 1820, to celebrate Caroline's 21st birthday, the entire village processed down to The Vyne, headed by the school children and the band, to enjoy a magnificent feast that she herself had provided - a memorable occasion for them, and, for Caroline, '*the happiest day of my life*'. She meant genuinely to do her best for the poor, of whom and whose circumstances she was all too well aware. In this she had been set a fine example by her aunt, who, as Wiggett puts it, 'was devoted to the poor', her acts of charity being 'constant and numerous'.

CHAPTER FIVE

Epilogue: The Improbable Revolutionary

William John Chute died on 13 December 1824. He was buried with his brother Chaloner in St Andrew's Church, beneath the communion rails on the north side of the chancel. Despite his failings, he had been deeply loved. The shops were shut in Basingstoke as a mark of respect, and the whole county is said to have mourned his loss.

A year or two before, while in London, he had finally been prevailed upon to remove his pigtail. His friend, General Pole, had coaxed him, with difficulty, into Fox the hairdresser's shop, but he had been reluctant even as he took the chair. 'Why sir, it cannot last much longer,' said the coiffeur, 'there are but five hairs left, all the rest is ribbon!' Grudgingly William consented, and the fatal snip was administered. A Fox had had his revenge at last! It was almost, but not quite, the last of the pigtails. When Wiggett Chute entered Parliament in 1837, an old Gloucestershire M.P. called Shepherd was still wearing one, but he was 'I believe the very last to carry that respectable appendage'.

The process of shedding his pigtail was painful enough. William would have been discomfited, if not distressed, by the wider changes that occurred within ten years of his death - the coming of the railways, for example, and the Great Reform Act of 1832. In Sherborne St John, the medieval open fields were about to be enclosed and age-old farming practices abolished in favour of an efficient modern system. Communications were to be dramatically improved by the building of new roads. Most of the old houses in the village were to be swept away in an actual, not merely a symbolic breach with the past. There was to be, as an approving Austen-Leigh puts it, a general 'draining and letting in of air and sunshine to the dark places of the earth'. Less than two hundred years have passed since a bemused Sherborne St John, then a stagnant community of peasants speaking a language of their own, was tardily dragged into the modern world. There has been no looking back.

Sherborne's revolution was not immediate. The house and farm were left to Eliza for her life (she died in 1843). Caroline, who harboured lifelong feelings of insecurity, felt herself lucky to find a husband in the local doctor, Thomas Workman, 'of course a match considered greatly beneath my station in life, but only in a social point of view for he was the perfect gentleman in his address, and [an] excellent husband and father (for he was a widower)'. Their wedding in 1837 was 'the first aristocratic wedding that had taken place at Sherborne church since Lady Hicks's, Uncle C's eldest sister'. The couple lived at first in a house on the edge of Basingstoke which they had built themselves. Called 'Old Bramblys', it is now in the centre of town and still operating as a surgery. As well as being step-mother to 'seven delicate children', Caroline gave birth in 1838 to a 'darling baby' of her own, which, tragically, survived for only a month. After living on Guernsey for a while, she retired in 1859 to Winchester, and wrote her *Reminiscences* at the behest of her nephew, young Chaloner Chute. Having outlived her old friend, Edward Austen-Leigh (who married a niece of Mrs Chute, became Vicar of Bray and himself wrote memoirs of the Vine Hunt and of his aunt, Jane Austen), Caroline died in 1881, at the respectable age of 82.

The ultimate heir to the estates was William's brother, the Rev. Thomas Vere Chute, a man of an equally conservative disposition. It is said that he once called on some of his Norfolk tenants and noticed an upright piano (then newly invented) in their sitting room. 'What kind of churn is that?' he asked. Though he continued to live in Norfolk, Tom Chute promptly bought (from Mr Brocas) the grandest house in the village, Tally's, intending to fit it up as his Hampshire residence. As he was not in a position to maintain his brother's beloved foxhounds, they went to live with a new Master, Abraham Pole, at West Ham. Lest their origins should be forgotten, the pack has been known ever since as 'The Vine Hounds'. Tom Chute was never to live in Sherborne, though, and Tally's was still unrenovated at the time of his death, aged 55, in January 1827.

The bachelor parson was buried at South Moulton, near his Norfolk seat, on a bitterly cold afternoon, with snow on the ground. There was keen anticipation among the various legatees, who assembled afterwards at South Pickenham Hall to hear the reading of the will. The identity of the heir was a mystery. The interested parties included an assortment of relatives and Thomas's personal servant, who was soon to discover that he had been left a house on the estate and a pension. There followed a number of bequests to Chute's numerous cousins, the Ellises. Only half way through the second page was the residual heir finally revealed: Thomas left 'the remainder of my personal Estate of every kind and description ... to William Lyde Wiggett Esq. of the Middle Temple 2d son of my cozen Revd. James Wiggett of Crudwell County of Wilts. for his own benefit absolutely'. The bequest specifically included all Thomas's manors and lordships, and was free of any condition, except that Wiggett should immediately assume the name and arms of Chute in addition to his own.

Fond as he was of his relatives, Wiggett was appalled by their mismanagement of the estate. Though far from humourless, he was by nature more serious and intellectual. He faced a considerable task to put the Hampshire property in order. One of his first acts as lord was to convene a session of the Manor Court, which had been adjourned since 1789. Country estates such as that of the Chutes were legally administered and regulated by this method until 1925. For example, the court meeting in 1789 had decreed that 'no person is in future to turn out any sheep in the Common Field 'till the Corn is all carried'. In well run lordships, courts met at least annually. In Sherborne, it had been convened on only thirteen occasions since 1717.

Wiggett's next step, in cooperation with young Bernard Brocas (old Mrs Brocas's step-grandson), was to enact the enclosure of the parish, which they achieved in 1829. A good deal of land was exchanged to create 'order out of confusion'. For instance, Wiggett acquired Crane's Farm from Brocas as a straight swap with Hillend. The boundary between their respective estates was conveniently marked by a new road, Morgaston Road. Miles of new fencing was erected. There followed a general thinning of the trees that would have appalled old William. Many acres of woodland and coppice were grubbed out altogether. Neat new fields, divided by whitethorn hedges, were established in their place.

Wiggett then embarked on an ambitious programme of reconstruction, in anticipation of which he established (at Kiln Farm) his own brickyard and tilery. The first new building, a carpentry shop, arose on the site of Moth's Farm, which he had purchased. Later called Abbotsfield, its first occupants were Mrs Chute's old butler, Wood, and his sons. They were succeeded by Dangerfield, 'a capital workman'. Manor Farm was to be Wiggett's first renovated farmhouse, followed in the ensuing years by Kiln, Weybrook, Popley Field, Vyne Lodge and Park Prewett. Scores of old buildings, such as the clerk's cottage in the churchyard and the outlying cottages at Pollard's End, were pulled down. Whilst the clerk was rehoused in one of the smart new cottages opposite, other displaced villagers, including 'many of the worst and most idle characters in the parish', were encouraged to emigrate. A batch of 25 went out to Canada in 1835, their expenses being paid by the parish, followed by a second wave in 1836, at the cost of the Chutes. Their emigration is described, not unjustly, as 'much to their own benefit and the relief of the parish'.

Wiggett demolished the ancient Rectory House in about 1840 and installed the then curate in Tally's, which became the new Rectory. The nucleus of the present school and the adjacent master's house were erected on the vacant site. The death of Mrs Bush, the former schoolmistress, had enabled him to further his plans. Her two-storey house on the hill made way for the present building (said to incorporate Gothic windows removed from the north wall of the church), designed as single-room accommodation for four old people. The thatched schoolroom next to it was converted into a further three tenements for the elderly. The brook at the bottom of the hill was covered over, as was that at the foot of Swingate Hill. 'Old Gage who had been footman at the Vyne for many years, fell in the water of the latter brook probably in a fit,' writes Wiggett, 'and although it was very shallow, he could not lift himself out of it and was suffocated. This happened in I believe the year 1832.'

If there were some in the village who found these changes unsettling, there is no record of it. On the contrary, William Clift describes Wiggett as 'a good landlord. He was truly one of the fine old English gentlemen, and was highly respected by all who lived around him. He would help the young and consider the old. I was often meeting him humming a tune and swinging his stick in his hand, and I had ample opportunity of well knowing him.' Wiggett maintained that, although he had pulled down many old cottages, he had 'altogether built a greater number to supply their places'. With their characteristic false windows and attractive brickwork, they are still to be seen throughout the parish. A typical Victorian reformer, Wiggett was interested in social control. Thus the Pollard's End cottages had been deemed 'a nest of very bad old cottages ... a long way from the Church and school, and a nuisance to everyone'. All available cottages, not already in his possession, were eagerly bought up. His purchases 'were all old and have nearly all been pulled down and rebuilt. I wished to have them in my own hands for the benefit of my labourers and to prevent the establishment of a beershop.' The new cottages were provided, on principle, with no more than two bedrooms. 'If there be three, the girl Sarah does *not* go out into service, though she is always on the point of going; or the young man John marries and stays on, with the young wife and baby in the old people's house, instead of getting one for himself.' Wiggett alludes however to 'the attraction of the rural population to large towns', and to 'the occupation of many cottages by old people whose children have married and settled elsewhere'. Despite having effected a social and economic revolution in the parish, to its general advantage, he was to witness a relentless decline in its population.

Unable to occupy The Vyne during the lifetime of his aunt, Wiggett was faced at her death with the considerable challenge of repairing it. The expenses were met by his sale of the Norfolk property in 1844. The following year, he took up residence at last, and from 1847, having retired from Parliament, was able to devote his entire attention to Sherborne St John. 'I cannot say of the buildings on the property what Augustus did of Rome, that he found it of stone and left it of marble, but I may say that I have converted them from rubble and rubbish and thatch into brick and mortar and tiles.' Those who have occupied them since have no doubt been grateful for the improvement. Most are now in private hands, having been sold by Wiggett's grandson, the future Sir Charles Chute, at a great post-war sale in 1919. Restrictive covenants permitting, they have generally been extended into three- or four-bedroomed houses, and command high prices that, a mere two hundred years ago, would have been beyond the wildest dreams of Sherborne cottagers.

Acknowledgments

The impetus behind this book was a talk given in Sherborne St John Village Hall in September 2001. The author thanks the Village Hall Management Committee and particularly Mrs Susan Burlingham who have so flatteringly and enthusiastically supported the venture. For their encouragment or help with his research, the author is further indebted to the following: Mr James Bromhead, Major John Bromhead, Mr. Ian Burlingham, Mr A.L. Cox, Headmaster of Sherborne St John School, Mrs Peggy Drury, Mr. and Mrs Anthony Greayer, Mr Stan Harmsworth, Mr and Mrs Michael Hillier, Mr Jonathan Ingram, property manager at The Vyne, Mr and Mrs Pat Linford, Mrs Metty Mackenzie, the Hon. Dwight Makins, Mr and Mrs Christopher Meredith, Mrs Sheila Millard, Miss Grace Monger, Mr Edward Roberts, Miss Amanda Russell of the NTPL, Mrs Rosemary Rust, Mrs Elizabeth Scott, and other National Trust staff members at The Vyne, Mrs John Seton, Mrs Jane Shelvey, Mr Nigel Smith, Dr John Teall and Mrs Christopher Willoughby. As always, the author's greatest debt is to his wife, Josephine, for her expert literary criticism and for being a continual inspiration.

Select Bibliography

'Aesop', *Sporting Reminiscences of Hampshire from 1745 to 1862* (London, 1864).

Anon., 'History of The Vyne', *The Topographer,* II (May 1789).

Montagu Burrows, *The Family of Brocas of Beaurepaire and Roche Court, Hereditary Masters of the Royal Buckhounds* (London, 1886).

Chaloner W. Chute, *A History of The Vyne in Hampshire* (Winchester and London, 1888).

Devereux W. Chute, *Jubilee Address* (privately printed, 1915).

W.L. Wiggett Chute, *Reminiscences of The Vyne House and Property* (1872), Hampshire Record Office ref. 31 M57/1072, 1073.

Sir William Cope, *A Glossary of Hampshire Words and Phrases* (1883).

Christopher Currie, *The Vyne Estate, Sherborne St John: An Archaeological Survey,* 3 vols. (1994).

Edward Edwards, T*he Life of Sir Walter Ralegh,* 2 vols. (London, 1868).

G.N. Godwin, *The Civil War in Hampshire (1642-45) and the Story of Basing House* (1904).

Moira Grant, 'The Alien Benedictine Priory of Monk Sherborne, Hampshire, from the Twelfth to the Fifteenth Centuries', *Proceedings of the Hampshire Field Club and Archaeological Society,* LV (2000).

Maurice Howard, *The Vyne, Hampshire* (The National Trust, 1998).

Jane Austen's Letters, collected and edited by Deirdre Le Faye (Oxford, 1996).

Trevor Lummis and Jan Marsh, *The Woman's Domain: Women in the English Country House* (London, 1990).

The Reminiscences of William Clift of Bramley (Basingstoke, 1908).

'A Sexagenarian' [James Edward Austen-Leigh], *Recollections of the Early Days of the Vine Hunt* (privately printed, 1865).

Claire Tomalin, *Jane Austen: A Life* (London, 1997).

The Victoria County History of Hampshire, ed. W. Page, Vol. IV (London, 1911)

Rev. John Wilkinson, 'Farming in Hampshire', *Journal of the Royal Agricultural Society of England,* XXII (1861).

A.T. Woods, *Sherborne St John: Notes, Jottings, History, Facts, and General Interesting Things in and around the Village, some old, some new* (unpublished MS, *c.* 1975).

Caroline Workman, *Reminiscences of Life at The Vyne* (1869-70), Hampshire Record Office ref. 31 M57/1070.

Index

By the same author . . .

SELBORNE: GILBERT WHITE'S VILLAGE

'A real treat ... it brilliantly conveys a sense of Selborne's development from the Middle Ages to the present day ... Well-written and beautifully presented, this is an example of local history at its best.'

Mark Page, *Hampshire Field Club and Archaeological Society Newsletter*

CHAWTON: JANE AUSTEN'S VILLAGE

'An excellent example of how a village guide can and should be written and produced'

The Coat of Arms

'Fascinating reading ... It would be very interesting to walk round the village with this book in hand'

Maggie Lane, *The Jane Austen Society Newsletter*

'Must surely become required reading for visitors to the village'

Hampshire Life

A KEY TO ODIHAM CASTLE

'The author draws upon both written and archaeological evidence to conjure up the medieval appearance and atmosphere of the castle'

Hampshire Chronicle